HOW TO ANALYZE PEOPLE

THE ULTIMATE GUIDE TO LEARN HOW TO SPEED READ PEOPLE, ANALYZE BODY LANGUAGE AND BECOME A HUMAN LIE DETECTOR

Table of Contents

Introduction

If you want to make sure you know what a person feels just by looking at her face, maybe it's time to understand a little more about body reading, which is nothing more than to realize that gestures and positions also have a lot to say - much more than you can imagine.

To give you an idea, 55% of the information a person relays when communicating comes from body language. This body reading thing is so curious that it is interesting to highlight some of the many types of research already done addressing the theme:

Did you know, for example, that psychopaths can detect vulnerability only by analyzing the way a person walks?

Another study suggests that it is possible to understand what a politician thinks about a particular subject solely based on his hands. Possible?

How To "Read" Someone

Typically, you are wondering how one person interprets the other through body language. You must be aware of the unconscious signals issued by your interlocutor, without them knowing that they are being analyzed. The three key points of body language are:

Speech and Behavior: To tell if a person feels emotionally attuned to you, notice if they use the same words as you; they speak in a tone and at a speed similar to the ones you use to talk; if they are sitting in the same position as you. If the conversation continues at a pace that makes it sound like a "follow the master" game, the emotional connection between both of you is adequately established;

Levels of agitation and activity: If the person does not move, he or she has little interest in what you have to say however if they run out after the meeting, it indicates that they are excited. Several surveys have already confirmed that when a woman swings her feet while on a romantic date, she probably likes the man she is with.

Emphasis and timing: The term "timing" means that the person is speaking or doing the right thing at the right time. If in addition to having a schedule for the relevant comments, the person emphasizes specific points, it means that they are focused and controlled. On the other hand, a person that does not show security in what he speaks, due to lack of timing and emphasis, is easily manipulated.

Still, on the quest for excellence in body language, you need to pay close attention to the interlocutor. In that sense, there are biases that you must analyze to improve your ability to perceive:

Think of the context: Would people in this situation act in the same way that the person who is talking to you is acting?

Look for joint, non-isolated actions: Do not focus on just one detail or gesture. Always observe the entire body.

Compare: How Does This Person Act Normally?

Know that your prejudices can deceive you. To understand the other, you need to understand yourself: see if you are not drawing conclusions because you like or because you do not like the person.

The way the human body communicates is often the subject of research, and scientists have come up with some rather curious specific conclusions about body language:

Crossed legs are a bad sign during negotiations. It sounds bizarre, but business meetings end better when no one is cross-legged. Just to give you an idea, the analysis of 2,000 meetings showed that none of them ended well when at least one person was cross-legged.

Want to know if someone is lying or betraying your trust? Notice that during a conversation the person has these four attitudes: he leans on his hand, he leans on his face, he crosses his arms and he maintains a posture that is tilted somewhere, not erect. These isolated signs do not amount to much, but when presented together, they probably indicate lies and/or betrayal;

On the other hand, research has already proven that trustworthy people are emotionally expressive. Trust someone who is pleasing to all people, and not just to a specific group.

Concerning the hands: Gestures made with the palms down indicate power and the opposite is submission.

Men and women use different body languages at the time of seduction. Women start smiling, raising their eyebrows, lowering their eyelids quickly, and then look away. Next, almost without exception, they place their hands close to their mouths and smile or lick their lips.

Men, on the other hand, inflame the chest, jut their chin, arch their backs, make gestures with their hands and arms and make movements that can demonstrate confidence and call attention to their power.

The fact is that if you want to read the body language, you need to avoid falling into some common traps, after all, crossed arms do not always mean lack of interest. Here are a few common mistakes made by people trying to gauge how others communicate by gesture:

You cannot ignore the context: The idea that someone is with crossed arms does not mean that he or she is not interested. It could be that they are in an icy environment or if the chair in which he or she is sitting does not have an armrest.

Notice the entire picture: Some people become obsessed with the idea of body reading and end up focusing only on one point of analysis, when, in fact, the ideal scenario would be to observe the entire situation: if the person is sweating, how is the breath, if they touch their face and so on;

Realize standard behaviors: If a person is always bouncing, you do not need to analyze it. Now if the person is always bouncing and, from one moment to another, the behavior changes, then you need to pay attention;

Stay tuned for these details: just know that if you already like or dislike a person, it will affect the judgment you make of them. If the person compliments you or if you find her attractive, maybe your judgments about them are favorable, even if you do not realize it - things of the human unconscious.

So, did you already know that body language may end up revealing some information that we do not make clear through words?

Chapter 1. The Importance of Analyzing People

Your capacity to analyze people might determine whether you will succeed or fail. Human beings are social animals. We almost always need the input of other human beings in order to achieve our important life goals. But what happens if we take on people that are unfit for their roles? We suffer defeat. Thus, it is of utmost importance to be able to analyze people. The following are some of the benefits of analyzing people.

It helps you know your allies

Whether you like it or not, the entire world will not take a liking to you. Some people will be for you, and other people will be against you. In order to maximize your chances of success, you must work with people who like you, while ignoring those who dislike you. Your capability to analyze people will help you single out those who are in favor of you. Considering that people can be pretty complex, your capability to understand their true persona cannot be overstated. For instance, if you're pursuing a career that involves serving the public, you will find yourself surrounded by all sorts of people. Clearly, not all of those people wish you well. Nevertheless, in the same breath, not all of them are against you. In such a situation, you have to exercise a lot of care, lest you end up working with your enemy who will eventually bring you down. If you tell your secrets to the enemy, he will run out there and spill it all. If you get close enough to the enemy, he might sow bad thoughts into your mind, which will see you taking the wrong direction. All of these can be avoided by sharpening your capability to tell good people apart from bad people. Of course, this is not a skill you can develop overnight. You have to practice repeatedly until you are good at spotting the fake ones.

It helps avoid conflict

In most cases, conflict arises because of a disparity in expectations. In a relationship, if the man expects one thing from his mate, and his wish is never met, it can cause him grief. And the vice versa is true. These are the kind of scenarios that cause conflict in a relationship. If the man had taken the time to understand what their partner is really like, they would not be shocked at a later time, when their partner behaved a certain way. Thus, it is important to understand the person that you're getting into a relationship with, for this will minimize your fights. Analyzing a person helps you understand their triggers. You get an opportunity to decide whether or not you want to involve yourself with them. If you're looking for a life partner, there are some things that you cannot compromise on, and so you must analyze potential candidates to find out whether or not they possess these characteristics. If you ignore this step, you are at risk of having a tumultuous marriage. Understanding what other people's personalities are like is a form of educating yourself on how to act or not act in front of these people. When you learn that someone is not into corny jokes, you will stop yourself from acting in a corny way, and in the same breath, when you realize that someone has a very fun attitude, you will try not to be a bore.

It allows you to appreciate diversity

Human beings are incredibly diverse. And this is a good thing. You cannot really understand this diversity until you pay attention to other people. Someone who comes from Asia might exhibit certain personality traits that differ from the average American. This is not a chance to bash the Asian for being different than you, but rather, it is an opportunity to appreciate the uniqueness of the Asian. People who bash others for being different than them are simply narrow-minded. Analyzing people gives you the power to recognize and accept our differences. It makes you a more cultured person. If you travel to other parts of the world, you will easily fit in because you have a mindset of adjusting. On the other hand, someone who is opposed to the recognition and appreciation of diversity will find himself at loggerheads with people who are unlike him.

It helps you fine-tune your goals

We don't live in a vacuum. The actions, words, and behaviors of other people will affect us. Every person has an idol that they look up to. Your idol is the person that you would want to trade lives with. Apart from giving you hope; your role model gives you an opportunity to study the various qualities that you will require in that line of work. For instance, if you want to become a journalist, you must know that it is not just about having language skills, but you must improve your personality, so that more people will not only be comfortable around you, enough to open up and let out their secrets. When you take on the practice of keenly observing other people, you are in a position to determine which career path suits your qualities.

It helps you understand the motivations of people

At the end of the day, there's a motive behind every action, but these motives are not always obvious. Some people will instantly reveal who they are, but there are people who will try to downplay their real image. But if you're a good observer, you can always tell what is going on. By taking your time to analyze people, you are in a much better position to understand what their goals are. Having this knowledge helps you take self-preserving decisions. Manipulative people are known for acting or speaking in a way that won't betray their manipulative agenda. Unless you are extra careful in your analysis of their persona, you might miss their motive, and become another one of their victims.

It helps you to understand a person's strengths

Every human being has both weaknesses and strengths. The reason why some of us become successful is that we capitalize on our strengths. Failure to capitalize on our strengths can make us feel disillusioned about life. The skill of identifying our strengths is important in identifying other people's strengths. Thus, when you are looking for someone to work with, you will be in a position to identify their strengths and weaknesses, which will make your team of high quality.

It helps in predicting behavior

Your capability to analyze personalities is vital in predicting how various people will act under different circumstances. Life is not one smooth ride. There are many challenges encountered on the road. In addition, for the most part, success depends on how we handle challenges. Being able to analyze various personalities empowers you to understand how people will react to challenges. For instance, if you notice that someone has the markings of a violent personality, or has anger issues, you might want to skip on that person because their violent nature will become soon apparent.

Chapter 2. How Can Anyone Speed Read People?

Understanding body language takes a lot of practice. You have first to ensure that you are aware of what different signals might mean. This can take some time, especially if you're not somebody who's always interacting with different people. What we have to understand as well is that the individuals that we are around the most will probably share a lot of the same body language as us. For example, if you're always hanging out with your sisters, brothers, mom, dad, and other family members, there's a good chance that you communicate with your body in the same way.

You were raised within that environment so of course; you're going to interact the same as well. Consider people who are like you. You might work in a tech office where everybody is a little bit more of an introvert. They might have the same body language as you as well.

What we have to consider is how different people from different cultures all throughout the world, of different ages, different genders, and so on will have various methods of body language. While we might be able to quickly understand the body language of the people that we know the closest, what we have to remember is that there is plenty we do not know about different people who aren't like us.

When it comes to speed reading, the most important thing to know is that we first should gather as much information about the situation as possible. This will include background knowledge on the individual, the context of the case, and the predictability factor for their different kinds of behaviors.

Once you're able to collect all of that relevant and useful knowledge, you can begin to apply it to their body language.

When it comes to how people use body language, it is a group signal. What this means is that there's not one singular thing that they do that will indicate how they act. It's an entire situation.

Somebody might have crossed arms. But if they have crossed arms, a shocked expression, and are a little standoffish, then they might just be trying to process that information. Somebody with a furrowed brow, a negative looking face, crossed arms, and an aggressive posture is going to be a little angrier. You might just see the crossed arms and think right away that they are closed off. However, there's going to be a deeper meaning in this action based upon all the other factors within the group signal. To speed read, what you'll want to do is look them up and down from top to bottom. Instantly connect all of the different aspects, and from there, you'll be able to make your conclusion. Speed reading body language revolves around the idea that we pick up on this group.

You don't want just to try to analyze that. You will consider all factors of the way that they're operating within a situation once you've been able to do this. You will then be able to discover that it's much easier to make conclusions surrounding their behavior.

Throughout this book, we are going to give you all the knowledge needed to understand best what others are trying to communicate with their bodies. By the end, it's going to be up to you to apply this. As a speed reader, you'll be able to scan them up and down like a computer and figure out based on all the different factors, what they might be trying to show you. Speed reading involves just taking the necessary and most straightforward forms and making a quick conclusion to really analyze somebody. You'll have to look deeper and deeper into their past and how they actually interact. As a speed reader, you're going to want to look at them quickly and make a conclusion, much like a snap of your fingers.

As you do this, it will be easier to understand all of the things that they might be trying to communicate with their bodies.

Chapter 3. Body Language Analysis

Being able to communicate well is extremely important when wanting to succeed in the personal and professional world, but it isn't the words you say that scream. It is your body language that does the screaming. Your gestures, posture, eye contact, facial expressions, and tone of voice are your best communication tools. These have the ability to confuse, undermine, offend, build trust, draw others in, or put someone at ease.

There are many times where what someone says and what their body language says is totally different. Non-verbal communication could do five things:

- Substitute – It could be used in place of a verbal message.
- Accent – It could underline or accent your verbal message.
- Complement – It could complement or add to what you are saying verbally.
- Repeat – It could strengthen and repeat your verbal message.
- Contradict – It could go against what you are trying to say verbally and make your listener think that you are lying.

We are going to cover:

Gestures – These have been woven into our lives. You might speak animatedly; argue with your hands, point, wave, or beckon. Gestures do change according to cultures.

Facial expressions – You will learn that the face is expressive and able to show several emotions without speaking one word. Unlike what you say and other types of body language, facial expressions are usually universal.

Eye contact – Because sight tends to be our strongest sense for most people, it is an important part of Non-verbal communication. The way someone looks at you could tell you whether they are attracted to you, affectionate, hostile, or interested. It might also help the conversation flow.

Body movement and posture – Take a moment to think about how you view people based on how they hold their head, stand, walk around, and sit. The way a person carries their self gives you a lot of information.

Non-verbal communication could go wrong in several different ways. It is very easy to confuse different signals and the rest of this chapter will make sure that that won't happen.

Lower Body

The arms share a lot of information. The hands share a lot more, but legs give us the exclamation point and can tell us exactly what someone is thinking. The legs could tell you if a person is open and comfortable. They could also tell you who dominance or where they want to go.

Legs Touching

When a person is standing, they will only be able to touch their bottom or thighs. This can be done seductively or they slap their legs as if they are saying "Let's go." It might also indicate irritation. This is when you have to pay attention to the context of the conversation. This is very important.

Pointing Feet

Look at the direction of a person's feet to see where their attention is. Their feet will always point toward what is on their mind or what they are concentrating on. Everyone has a lead foot and it all depends on their dominant hand. If the person talking is someone we are interested in, our lead foot will be pointing toward them. But, if they want to leave the situation, you will notice their foot pointing toward an exit or the way they want to go. If a person is sitting during the conversation, look at where their feet are pointing to see what they are truly interested in.

Smarty Pants

This is a position where someone tries to make themselves look bigger. They will usually be seated with their legs splayed open or leaning back. They might even spread their arms out and lock them behind their head. This is normally used by people who feel dominant, superior, or confident.

Shy Tangle

This is usually something that women do more than men. Anyone who begins to feel shy or timid will sometimes entangle their legs by crossing them under and over to try to block out bad emotions and to make themselves look smaller. There is another shy leg twirl that people will do when they are standing. The actual act of this movement is crossing one leg over the other and hooking that foot behind their knee as if they are trying to scratch an itch.

Upper Body

Upper body language can show signs of defensiveness since the arms could easily be used as a shield. Upper body language could involve the chest. Let's look at some upper body language.

Leaning

If someone leans forward, it will move them closer to another person. There are two possible meanings to this. First, it will tell you that they are interested in something, which could just be what you are talking about. But, this movement could also show romantic interest. Second, leaning forward could invade a person's personal space; hence, this shows them as a threat. This is often an aggressive display. This is done unconsciously by powerful people.

The Superman

This is commonly used by bodybuilders, models, and it was made popular by Superman. This could have various meanings depending on how a person uses it. Within the animal world, animals will try to make themselves look bigger when they feel threatened. If you look at a house cat when they get spooked, they will stretch their legs and their fur stands on end. Humans also have this, even if it isn't as noticeable. This is why we get goosebumps. Because we can't make ourselves look bigger, we have to come up with arm gestures like putting our hands on our waist. This shows us that a person is getting ready to act assertively.

This is normal for athletes to do before a game or a wife who is nagging their spouse. A guy who is flirting with a girl will use this to look assertive. This is what we call a readiness gesture.

The Chest in Profile

If a person stands sideways or at a 45-degree angle, they are trying to accentuate their chest. They might also thrust out their chest, more on this in a minute. Women do this posture to show off their breasts and men will do this to show off their profile.

Outward Thrust Chest

If someone pushes their chest out, they are trying to draw attention to this part of their body. This could also be used as a romantic display. Women understand that men have been programmed to be aroused by breasts. If you see a woman pushing her chest out, she might be inviting intimate relations. Men will thrust out their chest to show off their chest and possibly trying to hide their gut. The difference is that men will do this to women and other men.

Hands

Human hands have 27 bones and they are a very expressive part of the body. This gives us a lot of capability to handle our environment.

Reading palms isn't about just looking at the lines on the hands. After a person's face, the hands are the best source for body language. Hand gestures are different across cultures and one hand gesture might be innocent in one country but very offensive in another.

Hand signals may be small but they show what our subconscious is thinking. A gesture might be exaggerated and done using both hands to show a point.

Control

If a person is holding their hand with their palms facing down, they might be figuratively holding onto or restraining another person. This could be an authoritative action that is telling you to stop now. It might be a request asking you to calm down. This will be apparent if someone places their dominant hand on top of a handshake. If they are leaning on their desk with their palms flat, this shows dominance.

If their palms face outward toward another person, they might be trying to fend them off or push them away. They might be saying "stop, don't come closer."

If they are pointing their finger or their entire hand, they might be telling someone to leave now.

Greeting

Our hands get used a lot to greet other people. The most common way is with a handshake. Opening up the palm shows they don't have any weapons. This gets used when saluting, waving, or greeting others.

During this time, we get to touch another person and it might send various signals.

Dominance can be shown by shaking hands and placing the other hand on top. How long and how strong they shake the hand will tell you that they are deciding on when to stop the handshake.

Affection could be shown with the duration and speed of the handshake, smiles, and touching with the other hand. The similarity between this one and the dominant one could lead to a situation when a dominant person will try to pretend they are just being friendly.

Submission gets shows by placing their palms up. Floppy handshakes that are clammy along with a quick withdrawal also show submission.

Most handshakes use vertical palms that will show equality. They will be firm but won't crush and for the right amount of time so both parties know when they should let go.

Waving is a great way to greet people and could be performed from a long distance.

Salutes are normally done by the military, where a certain style is prescribed.

Holding

A person who has cupped hands shows they can hold something gently. They show delicacy or holding something fragile. Hands that grip will show desire, possessiveness, or ownership. The tighter the fist, the stronger they are feeling a specific emotion.

If someone is holding their own hands, they are trying to comfort themselves. They could be trying to restrain themselves so they will let somebody else talk. It could be used if they are angry and it is stopping them from attacking. If they are wringing their hands, they are feeling extremely nervous.

Holding their hands behind their back will show they are confident because they are opening up their front. They may hide their hands to conceal their tension. If one hand is gripping the other arm, the tighter and higher the grip, the tenser they are.

Two hands might show various desires. If one hand is forming a fist but the other is holding it back, this might show that they would like to punch somebody.

If someone is lying, they will try to control their hands. If they are holding them still, you might want to be a bit suspicious. Remember that these are just indicators and you should look for other signals.

If someone looks like they are holding onto an object like a pen or cup, this shows they are trying to comfort themselves. If a person is holding a cup but they are holding it very close and it looks like they are "hugging" the cup, they are hugging themselves. Holding onto any item with both hands shows that they have closed themselves off from others.

Items might be used as a distraction to release nervous energy like holding a pen but they are clicking it off and on, doodling, or messing with it. If their hands are clenched together in front of them but they are relaxed, and their thumbs are resting on each other it might be showing pleasure.

Shaping

Our hands have the ability to cut our words into the air to emphasize the things we say and their meanings. We are trying to create visualization.

If a man is trying to describe the fish he caught during his fishing trip, he might try to show the shape by indicating it with his hands. He might also carve out a certain shape that he wants his ideal mate to be. Other gestures might be cruder when they hold specific body parts and move sexually.

Face

People's facial expression could help us figure out if we trust or believe what they are saying. The most trustworthy expression will have a slight smile and a raised eyebrow. This expression will sow friendliness and confidence.

We make judgments about how intelligent somebody is by their facial expressions. People who have narrow faces with a prominent nose were thought to be extremely intelligent. People who smile and have joyous expressions could be thought of as being intelligent rather than someone who looks angry.

Mouth

Mouth movements and expressions are needed when trying to read body language. Chewing on their lower lip might indicate a person who is feeling fearful, insecure, or worrying.

If they cover their mouth, this might show that they are trying to be polite if they are yawning or coughing. It might be an attempt to cover up disapproval. Smiling is the very best signal, but smiles can be interpreted in many ways. Smiles can be genuine or they might be used to show cynicism, sarcasm, or false happiness.

Watch out for the following:

Their lips are pursed.

If a person tightens their lips it might be a sign of distaste, disapproval, or distrust.

They bite their lip.

People will bite their lip if they are feeling anxious, worried, or stressed.

They cover their mouth.

If a person tries to hide a reaction, they might cover their mouth to hide a smile or a smirk.

Their mouth is turned up or down.

Changes in the mouth that are subtle might be a sign of how the person is feeling. If their mouth is turned up a little bit, they might be feeling happy or optimistic. If their mouth is turned down, they could be feeling sadness, disapproval, or grimacing.

Negative Emotions

The silent signals that you show might harm your business without you even knowing it. We have over 250,000 facial signals and 700,000 body signals. Having poor body language could damage your relationships by sending other person signals that you can't be trusted. They might turn off, alienate, or offend other people.

You have to keep your body language in check and this takes a lot of effort. Most of the time, you may not know that you are doing it and you might be hurting your business and yourself.

In order to help you manage your signals, there are several body languages and speech mistakes that you can learn to prevent. Here are some mistakes that you can avoid:

Not Enough Response

If you are talking with someone, you need to make sure you listen to them. This means you have to smile, nod, and make eye contact. Even if two people don't agree with what each other are saying, you need to let them know that you have heard what they said. This is showing them respect. If you don't do this, you will leave a bad impression.

Using the Word "But"

Constantly using the word "but" while you are talking can cause many problems. Most of the time, this will sound like you are just trying to make up some excuses or you don't care about what they are saying. You might say: "I am sorry that your product didn't get to you on time, but you know how the weather is." This statement doesn't show you are sorry. You are placing the blame on the weather instead of addressing the real problem.

Personal Space

Invading another person's personal space can have detrimental results. One good example is men who always seem to invade a woman's personal space whether they know it or not. This could cause some harassment lawsuits. The best space to keep between you and others is about one and a half feet. Never treat another person's space as if it was your own.

Talking Too Fast

Blinking fast or talking too quickly shows nervousness and distrust. Try to pause between each sentence and let others finish their sentence before your interrupt. Eye contact is very important. If you have a hard time looking people in the eye, look in the center of their forehead. It looks like eye contact without all those uncomfortable feelings.

Not Listening

It doesn't matter what you do for a living, you are going to have to talk with people some time or another. The main thing that will make or break any relationship is not listening. Listening could impact your relationship with employees, suppliers, performance, and sales better than any other form of communication.

Slumping

If a person slumps in their seat, they show that they don't have any energy or confidence. It is important to show passion and let others know that you believe in yourself. If you are hunched over or slumping, you are sending the wrong message. If your posture is strong, you are going to feel energetic and it will be a win for all people involved.

Checking Your Phone

If you are in a public gathering, put away your phone. Everybody is addicted to their phones now, and this is extremely rude. Try engaging with others and stop checking your phone every few minutes. If you have an emergency, that's fine. It is easier to make connections with others if you don't have things distracting you.

Face is Scrunched-Up

You might not realize that your face is scrunched-up or that your brow is furrowed. This can help others think you are intimidating or hostile. You can discourage others from being open or it might make them get defensive. You can verbally assure them that you understand and support what they are saying.

Not Making Eye Contact

I used to work with someone who would immediately stare into space anytime someone talked to them. They claimed it was easier for them to focus on what others were saying if they didn't look at who was talking. People might use many different communication types but always make eye contact. Even if you can keep moderate eye contact, it will communicate confidence, interest, and will put everybody at ease.

Not Smiling

Do you know that smiling can make you feel happy? People like to believe the opposite. If you can keep a nice smile on your face, you will feel more confident and people will want to work with you. If you realize you want to make a face, turn that face into a smile.

Glancing Around

Everybody has encountered someone who will constantly look around while they are talking to you. It probably makes you think that they are trying to find someone else to talk to. Don't be this person. Everyone you talk to needs to be treated with respect.

Handshake Too Weak or Strong

Handshakes are normally the first impression that someone gets from you. If your handshake is too weak, it will show that you aren't professional and it might be new to them. If your handshake is too strong, it might warn them that you are being too aggressive. Try to find a happy medium so that you will make a good impression.

When you observe other people carefully, you can pick up on their emotions by their Non-verbal signals. These indicators are not a guarantee. Contextual clues might be used, in addition to what they are saying and what is happening around you at the time.

Chapter 4. Common Facial Signals for Different Emotions

The expression facial (also, facies, face), with the eyes, is one of the most important means to express emotions and moods.

Through knowledge and observation of facial expressions (that is, the moving face and not as a static object) we can get a better understanding of what others communicate to us.

We also make judgments about people's personality and other traits based on what we see in their faces. For example, people with attractive features are often attributed certain qualities that they may or may not actually possess.

Not all communication that is transmitted through facial expression is susceptible to being consciously perceived by the interlocutor; however, it is known that the impressions we get from others are also influenced by the imperceptible movements of their verbal communication.

The face and first impressions

In a first meeting between two people, the first five minutes are usually the most critical period. The impressions formed in this short space of time will tend to persist in the future, and even be reinforced by subsequent behavior, which is not usually interpreted objectively, but according to those first impressions.

Since the face is one of the first features we notice in a person, it can clearly play a vital role in the process of establishing relationships with others.

In these few minutes we form opinions about your character, personality, intelligence, temperament, ability to work, about your personal habits, even about your convenience as a friend or lover.

Talking to the face

Together with the eyes, the face is our best means to communicate without words. We use it (and the judgments of others will depend on the clues they get) to indicate how pleasant we are as people, to express our current state of mind, to show the attention we pay to others, and so on. However, facial expressions can be used to reinforce the impact of verbal messages, such as when a mother scolds her child: the expression on her face will show if she is really angry, or only a little...

The main function of the face in body language is the expression of emotions; although other parts of the body also contribute to the use we make of body language, so we should not believe that a message is clear and exclusively transmitted by a single part of the body.

The range of expressions is very wide, but there are a limited number of emotions that most of us can recognize with some reliability.

Paul Ekman and Wallace Friesen, have discovered that there are 6 main facial expressions:

The smiles

The smiles can be light, normal, and large. They are usually used as a gesture of greeting, to express varying degrees of pleasure, joy, happiness, etc. Even blind-born children smile when they like something. They are characterized by being beautiful and cheerful. Smiles can also be used to mask other emotions:

- Smiles can be used to hide the hardships.
- Smile can be a submission response.
- Smiles can make stressful situations more bearable.
- Smiles can attract the smiles of others.
- Smiles sometimes are used to relax the tension.
- Smile can be used to hide fear.

Sadness, disappointment and depression

They are distinguished by lack of expression and by features such as: downward inclination of the corners of the mouth, low gaze and general decay of the factions. Normally these emotions are accompanied by a low volume of the voice or a slower way of speaking.

Although in most cases they are not very well distinguished from each other, there are other bodily factors that give us the assurance of knowing which emotion is being carried out as:

Sadness

- Eyebrows slightly tilted towards the ears forming a semiarch.
- Shoulders regularly decayed.
- Inclination of the commissures at 45% of their normal range.
- Hands together and face down.
- Disappointment.
- Eyebrows not fully inclined.
- Looking back, and down, usually to the left.
- Shoulders slightly down and with the hands at the sides of the body.

Depression

- Normally inclined eyebrows.
- Tilt of the commissures slightly descending.
- Shoulders totally down.
- Legs and thighs parallel to each other.
- But we must remember that each emotion is different according to each individual. Not everyone demonstrates the same factions.

Dislike / contempt

They express themselves with shrinkage of the eyes and puckering of the mouth. The nose is usually wrinkled and the head turned sideways to avoid having to look at the cause of such a reaction. It is the only facial expression that occurs in only part of the face, that is, in the middle of it. One end of the upper lip is lifted while the opposite side is in its original position.

Anger

The anger is often characterized by: gaze into the cause of the offense, closed mouth and teeth tightly clenched, eyes and eyebrows slightly inclined to express anger. Closed hands pressing and containing the feeling can also be seen in a situation of anger.

The fear

The fear is not a unique form of expression that reveals its presence. It can be revealed through very wide eyes, through the open mouth or by a general tremor that affects the face and the rest of the body.

The interest

It is often detected by what is called "bird head", that is, the head tilts a certain angle towards the subject of interest. Other features are: eyes more open than normal and mouth slightly open.

Another aspect to consider is the extent to which the complements in nonverbal messages are involved. Because the complements change our appearance, we must take into account their effects on the perception that others have of us. From this it can be deduced that we do not always transmit the nonverbal messages we try to send. The more aware we are of these difficulties of body language, without words, the better we can use it.

Other information about the face

Facial expressions, in addition to expressing emotions, also serve as a means of expressing personality, attitudes towards others, sexual attraction and attractiveness, the desire to communicate or initiate an interaction and the degree of expressiveness during communication.

Differences have been found in the way men and women use facial expressions to communicate. Women tend to laugh and smile more often than men, which does not have to be due to greater sociability or joy, it may be because they find the situation slightly uncomfortable.

The expression of the face is constantly changing during communication. Among the changes we can mention the so-called "micro momentary" facial expressions, as its name indicates its duration is a fraction of a second and usually reflects the true feelings of a person.

Laughter

The laughter is a biological response produced by the body in response to certain stimuli. The smile is considered a soft and silent form of laughter. There are currently various interpretations about its nature.

The most recent studies, high impact, are made since 1999 by Robert Provine, a neurobiologist of the behavior of the University of Maryland, who said laughter is a "babbling playful, instinctive, contagious, stereotyped and control unconscious, or involuntary - which occurs rarely in solitude. In humans, laughter begins, on average, towards four months of age, and, according to recent scientific studies, it constitutes a form of innate communication inherited from primates and closely related to language.

On the other hand, for other authors, such as Charles R. Gruner, of the University of Georgia (1978), laughter is reminiscent or synonymous with the shout of triumph of the fighter after winning his adversary. Ensures that in all manifestations of humor there is a gesture of aggression, even in the most innocuous cases. According to Gruner, "even an infant laughs, not as a manifestation of thanks, but because he got what he wanted." The philosopher John Morreall (1983) argues that the biological origin of human laughter could be in a shared expression of relief after passing the danger; the laxity we feel after laughing can help inhibit the aggressive response, turning laughter into a sign of behavior that indicates trust in classmates.

In any case, there is recent research conducted both in orangutans and chimpanzees that suggest that they are able to laugh, which would make laughter of evolutionary and genetic origin.

It is popularly considered basically a response to moments or situations of humor, as an external expression of fun, and related to joy and happiness, although laughter, according to numerous studies, such as Robert Provine, is motivated by a comic stimulus in A minority of everyday cases. It usually appears, more or less simulated, as an emotional complement to verbal messages, as well as in situations of stress or in playful behaviors such as tickling.

Some medical theories attribute beneficial effects on health and well-being to laughter, since it releases endorphins.

Forms of laughter

Depending on the force with which it occurs, laughter can vary both in its duration and in its tone and characteristics. Thus, we use different words to describe what we consider different types of laughter: click, laugh, giggle, contemptuous, desperate, nervous, equivocal laughter. Other types: caquino, jingle, evil laugh, hypoid.

Among the emotional cues, the smile is the most contagious of all, and smiling encourages positive feelings. Like the laugh itself, the smile is innate, and deaf and blind children smile. It usually appears at six weeks of life and is the first language of the human being. Initially it is a physical behavior, and gradually evolves into an emotional behavior. Self-induction of the gesture of smiling can improve our mood. Another property is to induce an increase in the activity of NK cells and thus improve our immune status.

Some studies show that laughter varies by gender: women tend to laugh in a more singing way, while men tend to laugh more in a snorting or growling way.

Physiology of laughter

It occurs when a stimulus - internal or external - is processed in primary, secondary and multimodal association areas of the central nervous system. The processing of emotions is carried out in the limbic system, which is probably responsible for the potential motors that characterize laughter, including facial expression and the movements of the muscles that control ventilation and phonation. Once the stimulus has been processed, in addition to the aforementioned automatic motor acts, a generalized autonomous activation is carried out, which has an exit through several routes, among which are the Hypothalamus-pituitary axis and the autonomic nervous system. All these components make up the emotion, a process that involves, when it comes to joy, the motor act called laughter.

There are two structures of the limbic system involved in the production of laughter: the amygdala and the hippocampus.

Some studies

Laughter can be induced by stimulating the subthalamic nucleus, and it has been proven in patients with Parkinson's disease. A recent work by Itzhak Fried of the University of California, has allowed us to locate an area of the brain called a supplementary motor area, which, when stimulated by means of electrodes, produces the smile and, with a more intense stimulation, laughing out loud. The supplementary motor area is an area very close to the language area. This mechanism was discovered accidentally while treating a young woman with epilepsy.

Experiments have been conducted to determine exactly in which area the sense of humor resides. In a study, presented in 2000 by scientists at the University of Rochester, volunteers underwent functional magnetic resonance while asking them various questions. Their conclusions were that this characteristic resided in a small region of the frontal lobe. However, another London team performed the same test on individuals who were told jokes, and the results were that the brain area that was activated was the ventral prefrontal cortex along with other regions involved in the language process when the joke's grace resided in a pun.

Medical perspective

Children 7-10 years laugh around 300 times a day, while adults who still laugh do less than 80 times a day. There are people who rarely laugh, and even some people who don't feel the need to laugh.

Studies since the 1980s by Lee S. Berk demonstrated over several years the positive effects of laughter:

Some stress- related indicators decreased during laughter episodes, related to the decreased epinephrine and cortisone levels.

Laughter increased the production of antibodies and the activation of protective cells such as lymphocytes and cytotoxic T lymphocytes, which produce cellular immunity, important to prevent the formation of tumors.

Cheerful and repetitive laughter or laughter improved mood, reduced blood cholesterol levels and regulated blood pressure.

More recently (2010), Berk has discovered a relationship between laughter and appetite, so that laughter increases appetite analogously to how moderate physical exercise does. According to these studies, there is simultaneously a reduction in the level of leptin and an increase in ghrelin in the blood.

Other beneficial effects of laughter are as follows:

- Free from fear and anguish.
- It helps to calm the anger.
- It contributes to a change of mental attitude that favors the decrease of diseases.
- It promotes digestion by increasing the contractions of all abdominal muscles.
- It facilitates the evacuation due to the "massage" that it produces on the viscera.
- It increases the heart rate and pulse and, by stimulating the release of "endorphin" hormones, allows them to fulfill one of their important functions, such as maintaining the elasticity of the coronary arteries.
- It decreases the presence of cholesterol in the blood as it amounts to an aerobic exercise.
- It helps reduce blood glucose.

Robert Provine: laughter as communication

Popularly, laughter and smiling are associated with happiness and good humor; however they are not reliable measures of humor. According to recent studies, laughter is a communication mechanism. It follows that the triggering factor of laughter is not happiness or joy in themselves, but the fact that there is at least one other person who can receive the message, in the form of playful babble. It has been proven that the relationship between laughter in society and laughter in solitude is 30 to 1. Literally, we need more people, so they laugh and we laugh with them.

Field study

Provine sought to adopt a "naturalistic and descriptive tactic" to reveal the subconscious triggers and instinctive roots of laughter. He initially observed subjects in his laboratory, but found that laughter was too fragile, illusory and variable under direct scrutiny. Therefore, he decided to observe the appearance of natural and spontaneous laughter in daily life. He began to listen and secretly record the conversational laugh (the one that typically follows the conversation speech a second later), documenting 1200 episodes, and later studied the patterns of who laughed and when, to analyze their qualities. His conclusion was that in order for laughter to occur, more than one person is necessary, the minimum element being a dyad, a speaker and a listener (except in the case of a spectator laughing out loud watching television, for example). Laughter tended to follow a natural conversational rhythm, splashing the speech after complete statements, and especially after changes in volume or intonation. The most interesting thing was that less than a quarter of the previous comments were really humorous. Provine suggests that laughter synchronizes the brains of the speaker and the listener, in such a way that it serves as a signal for the receptive areas of language, perhaps switching the activation between competitive brain structures of cognition and emotion.

The observations of interpretation students laughing at the right time led him to conclude that laughter is under a relatively weak conscious control, and that the most natural-looking laughter is caused by subconscious mechanisms, which explains why method acting can lead to the reproduction of emotions more effectively.

Tickle and laugh

Probably, tickling is the oldest and safest way to stimulate laughter. Tickling and laughter are one of the first forms of communication between mother and baby. Laughter appears between three and a half to four months of life, that is, long before he speaks. For this reason, the mother uses the tickles to stimulate the baby's laughter and thus establish communication. Laughter in turn encourages the mother to continue to tickle, until there comes a time when the baby begins to complain, at which time the mother stops.

For the same fact that it is more difficult to laugh alone, it is also difficult for a person to tickle themselves. Tickling is an important part of the game, so when you tickle a person, you not only try to escape and laugh, but try to return them. In the process of giving and receiving tickles, there is a kind of neurological programming that causes people to establish links, and the same thing happens with sex. The armpits, the palms of hands and soles of the feet are areas whose stimulation by tickling produces laughter more easily.

Laughter is contagious

Like yawning, laughter is a neurologically programmed social behavior, whose origin lies in the need to synchronize the state of group behavior. It is, for example, why there is a hint of laughter in sitcoms on television. When we hear another person laugh at something, we immediately look at that something and consider it more fun than if that person does not laugh, and then we smile or even laugh.

Laughter and sex

Both men and women laugh to the same extent. However, the situation that produces the most laughter is when a man talks to a woman, or vice versa, and in this situation the woman is the one who leads the laughter and the man the leader of laughter production. As with speech, the laughter of women generally presents a more acute tone than that of men. One of the characteristics of the most attractive men for women is the sense of humor, although not precisely the ability to laugh. That is, the woman looks for a man who makes her laugh and does not laugh too much himself.

Laughter as a mechanism for controlling others

The relationship between laughter and world events is modulated by culture and society. Currently, we relate laughter to the idea of "being happy and feeling good." However, Plato and Aristotle, among other authors who wrote about laughter, had a darker view of this. They, for example, found public executions fun, something that is currently politically incorrect, just as they also laughed, in addition to the people in their group, people from other groups, such as other ethnicities or races. At present, our own language nuances such a difference: laughing at someone who is not the same is different than laugh at someone who isn't. For Robert Provine, ridiculous laughter is an ancestral instinctive mechanism different from group laughter that served to modulate the behavior of individuals who did not belong to the group itself, in order for them to adapt and integrate into it. The anthropologist Verena Alberti uses the terms "laughter of welcome" and "laughter of exclusion".

According to the scientist, that is the reason why people laugh in embarrassing or unpleasant circumstances. He affirms that laughter is an instrument to change the behavior of others. In an embarrassing situation, such as a dispute, laughter represents a gesture of appeasement, a way to lessen anger and tension. If the other person is infected, the risk of confrontation is dissipated.

Provine's observations suggested that social rank determines patterns of laughter, especially in the workplace; bosses easily provoke laughter from their subordinates and make jokes at their expense, suggesting that the phenomenon is generally a response to submission to the domain.

Laughter as the origin of language

According to Robert Provine, linguists and language scholars do not pay due attention to laughter, while physiology of the larynx and of various parts of the vocal pathways does play a part in the production of sound. In his own words:

"Laughter is part of the universal human vocabulary, and if we want to understand how the brain produces sound we should analyze behaviors that everyone has in the same way; that is, studying laughter - if we want to understand human behavior - will be like using E. coli, or the fruit fly, to understand the mechanism of genetics. Instead of facing the immense complexity of nature, we try to concentrate on a small molecule, which is a part, which can be better accessed." - Robert Provine.

Chapter 5. Posture and Body Orientation

Even though posture is affected by our health status and sometimes the furniture, in standard environments, our posture is largely mediated by our emotional states, and for this reason, body posture can help communicate more about an individual character, personality, and emotion. One of the advantages of body language is that it is hardly influenced by the conscious mind, and this makes body language a highly reliable source of profiling a person. We require reading body language so that we can ascertain the truth-value of the claims of an individual. If a person says that they are feeling sorry for what they did before you can accept their apologies, you will need to ascertain the honesty of that claim, and this is where reading body language comes in. As indicated, some professions such as medical, law enforcement, and conflict resolution require near accurate reading of an individual's body language.

As suggested, posture and body, orientation should be read in the context of the entire body language to develop the full meaning being communicated. Starting with an open posture, it is used to denote friendliness and positivity. In this open position, the feet are spread wide, and the palms of the hands are facing outward. Individuals with open posture are deemed more persuasive compared to those with other postures. To realize an open posture, one should stand up or sit straight with the head raised and keep the abdomen and chest exposed. When the open posture is combined with a relaxed facial expression and good eye contact, it makes one look approachable and composed. Maintain the body facing forward toward the other person during a conversation.

Regarding the closed posture, one crosses the arms across the chest, or crosses the legs away from someone or sits in a hunched forward position as well as showing the backs of the hands and clenching the fists, this is indicative of a closed posture. The closed posture gives the impression that one is bored, hostile, or detached. In this posture, an individual is acting cautious and appears ready to defend himself or herself against any accusation or threat. If this posture is exhibited in an audience, then the individual is feeling insecure by the message, the speaker, or due to the actions of another member of the audience.

Additionally, there is a confident posture that helps communicate that one is not feeling anxious, nervous, or stressed. The confident posture is attained by pulling oneself to full height, holding the head high, and keeping the gaze at eye level. Then pull your shoulders back and keep the arms as well as legs relaxed by the sides. The posture is likely to be used by speakers in a formal context such as when making a presentation, during cross-examination or in a project presentation.

One should always take note of the postural echoing when it is used as a flirting technique by attracting someone in the guardian. It is attained by observing and mimicking the style of the person and the pace of movement. When the individual leans against the wall, replicate the same. By adjusting your postures against the others to attain a match, you are communicating that you are trying to flirt with the individual. The postural echoing can also be used as a prank game to someone you are familiar with and often engage in casual talk with.

Sustaining a straight posture communicates confidence and formality. Part of the confidence of this posture is that it maximizes blood flow and exerts less pressure on the muscle and joints that enhances the composure of an individual. The straight posture helps evoke desirable mood and emotion that makes an individual feel energized and alert. A straight posture is highly preferred for informal conversations such as during meetings, presentations, or when giving a speech.

Relatedly being in a slumped position and hunched back is a poor posture and makes one be seen as lazy, sad, or poor. A slumped position implies a strain to the body that makes the individual feel less alert and casual about the ongoing conversation. On the other hand, leaning forward and maintaining eye contact suggests that one is listening keenly. During a speech, if the audience leans forward in an upright position, then it indicates that they are eager and receptive to the message.

In this manner, if one slants one of the shoulders when participating in a conversation, then it suggests that the individual is tired or unwell. Leaning on one side acutely while standing or sitting indicates that you are feeling exhausted or fed up with the conversation and are eagerly waiting for the end or a break. Think of how you or others reacted when a class dragged on to almost break time. There is a high likelihood that the audience slanted one of their shoulders to the left or right direction. In this state, the mind of the individual deviates to things that one will do next. In the case of a tea break, the mind of the students will deviate to what one will do during or after the tea break.

If one stands on one foot, then it indicates that one is feeling unease or tired. When one stands on one foot, it could also suggests that the person is trying to cope with some uncomfortable situation. The source of uneasiness could be emotional or physiological. For instance, you probably juggled your body from one foot to help ease the need to go for a short walk or to pass wind. In most cases, one finds himself or herself standing on one foot when an uncomfortable issue is mentioned.

It is a way to disrupt the sustained concentration that may enhance the disturbing feeling.

Furthermore, if one stands with their arms-akimbo while standing, then the individual is showing a negative attitude or disapproval of the message. The posture is created by holding the waist with both hands while standing up straight and facing the target person. The hands should simultaneously grip on the flanks, the part near the kidneys. In most cases, the arms-akimbo posture is accompanied by disapproval or sarcastic face to denote attitude, disdain, or disapproval.

Should one cup their head or face with their hands and rests the head towards the thighs, then the individual is feeling ashamed or exhausted. When the speaker mentions something that makes you feel embarrassed, then one is likely to cup their face or head and rest the face down towards the thighs. It is a literal way of hiding from shame. Children are likely to manifest this posture though they do it while standing. When standing this posture may make one look like he or she is praying.

If one stretches both of their shoulders, arms, and rests them on chairs on either side, then the individual is feeling tired and casual. The posture is akin to a static flap of wings where one stretches their shoulder and arms like wings and rests them on chairs on either side. It is one of the postures that loudly communicates that you are bored, feeling casual, and that you are not about the consequences of your action. The posture is also invasive of the privacy and space of other individuals and may disrupt their concentration.

Relatedly, if one bends when touching both of their knees, then the individual is feeling exhausted and less formal with the audience. The posture may also indicate extreme exhaustion and need to rest. For instance, most soccer players bend without kneeling while holding both of their knees, indicating exhaustion. Since in this posture, one is facing down, the posture may be highly inappropriate in formal contexts and may make one appear queer.

If one leans their head and supports it with an open palm on the cheeks, then it indicates that one is thinking deep and probably feeling sad, sorrowful, or depressed. The posture is also used when one is watching something with a high probability of negative outcomes such as a movie or a game. The posture helps one focus deep on the issue akin to meditating.

Similarly, crossing your arms to touch shoulders or touch the biceps indicates that one is deliberately trying to focus on the issue being discussed. Through this posture, an individual tries to avoid distractions and to think deeper on what is being presented. If you watch European soccer, you will realize that coaches use this posture when trying to study the match, especially where their team is down. However, this posture should not be used in formal contexts as it suggests rudeness. The posture should be used among peers only.

Lastly, there is the crossing of the legs from the thigh through the knee while seated on a chair, especially on a reclining chair. In this posture, one is communicating that he or she is feeling relaxed and less formal. In most cases, this posture is exhibited when one is at home watching a movie or in the office alone past working hours. If this posture is replicated in a formal context, then it suggests boredom or lack of concentration.

Finally, for the posture where one crosses the legs from the ankle to the soles of the feet while seated, it communicates that one is trying to focus on an informal context such as at home. For instance, if a wife or a child asks the father about something that he has to think through, then the father is likely to exhibit this posture. If this posture is replicated in a formal context, then it suggests boredom or lack of concentration.

Posture, and body orientation should be interpreted in the context of the entire body language to develop the full meaning being communicated.

Chapter 6. How to Fake Your Body Language

Faking body language is not easy because there is always something that is going to sell you out. It could be the eyes are not accompanying the smile, the hands are not accompanying the words, or the head is not following the hands and many other things. However, despite the entire sell out, body language faking can be learned so it means it is possible to fake your body language. You do not need to fake 100 percent of your body language because there will be a hitch, but you can always fake 70 percent of it. For you to fake your body language, you must first understand how to learn and interpret body language. It is like a basketball game, you cannot be good at basketball if you haven't learned about its rules, the risks involved, the importance of the game and the remedy if you are not achieving the expected results.

In body language faking, just like in the example above, you must know what your expectations are. Why are you faking it? You must know how good you are. This means you should try it on someone you know and ask them what they think. You must understand the body language you want to fake very well before attempting it otherwise it will shame you. Faking body language should be used for the common good rather than in a conspicuous way. When some people fake body language it boosts confidence in them and others. There are different ways you can fake your body language to suit your desires. Below are a few of the ways to do it;

Taking In A Deep Breath

When talking to someone whether you are giving a speech to an audience or you are listening to them, you should watch both the breathing rate and the other persons. The breathing rate of a person tells much about your emotions. Breathing of a person and his emotions are highly connected so you must be very careful with your rate of breathing if you want to fake it. When someone breaths deeply, it might show that he is afraid. A person holding his breath for some time and then breathing deeply shows that the person is afraid. For example, a child who knows that after telling his mother that he stole some candies knows he will be punished, no matter how his mother asks him; he will simply breathe deeply without speaking.

He is sending a message to his mother that he is afraid that if he speaks, he will be punished. So if you are afraid and you do not want to show the other person, you want to feel more superior, you want to prove that you are not afraid of doing anything or you are not afraid of the other person, make sure that your breathing rate is balanced. You should not breathe in deeply once after he has asked a question, take time breathing normally, you can hold your breath a little bit then start breathing normally, someone won't recognize the fear that you are experiencing.

Taking a deep breath may also signify anger. When someone is angry, he has no control over the thing or the one upsetting him. Just like fear, anger is emotional and like we said emotional feelings are connected to breathing. When you are so upset and so angry, watch your breathing rate if you do not want to show it. To fake your breathing rate, you can smile a bit and sip some water if there is any in the glass nearby instead of breathing deeply. Maintain your eye contact and think of funny things in your past, use humor, like crack a funny joke when the person aiming to make you angry says an awful thing, you can also repeat a calming phrase within your head like 'take it easy, take it easy, everything is fine'. This will help calm you down and you will realize your breathing rate is normal.

Deep breathing also shows excitement. This could be like the excitement after a party. You sit down and think about it, you hold your breath while thinking about it then you breathe in so deeply. You are excited that it was a wonderful party, but if you happened to sneak out of the house and go for this wonderful party and you come back to find your parents waiting for you, you have to fake it because a party on a school day is guaranteed to bring punishment. To fake it you should make sure you do not breathe deep in with a wide smile on your face. Not doing this will make your parents see your excitement and know what you were up to.

When someone is relieved, he is likely to take a deep breath. Thus taking a deep breath signifies relief. You may have been fighting with someone over a piece of land for a year, and then he comes to you and says that he has let it go, you can have it. This is a relief. You will take a deep breath after that. You can always fake this so that you can see how tiring the case was to you.

When you breathe in deeply, it might also show shock, surprise which is always accompanied by a head sign, love attraction, hopelessness or sadness. If you have to fake all these, you must make sure your breathing stays normal no matter how much these feelings flood your mind. To make sure you want to fake all your emotional traumas or feelings without anyone knowing they are fake; it is also good that you identify your emotional triggers. This will help you be in charge of your emotions and each time any trigger is pressed, you will find yourself smiling about it and it will not affect you. This way you would have faked it beyond any doubt.

Controlling the movement of your eyebrows

The eyebrow movement will tell what you are thinking and the message you are trying to pass across. By lowering your eyebrows when speaking to someone it will send a variety of messages. When your eyebrows are lowered, it shows deception. You will be concealing something from the audience or the speaker. If you want to fake this even if you are hiding something, make sure your eyebrows are raised humbly. This will send a different message. Lowered eyebrows also show desire. The desire that the eyes cannot see or are afraid to view. For example in a love relationship, when a partner asks for a kiss, you might find yourself lowering your eyebrows. This is sending a message that you have the desire to kiss but you can't say it, or the eyes can't help it. If you want to fake this so that the other person does not see that you have no desire, you can act surprised by raising your eyebrows with your eyes wide open or do exactly what is required. This will tell the person of your surprise or of your desires in the kiss too.

A person lowering eyebrows may also be annoyed. Annoyance may be caused by a variety of things and he is afraid that if he raises his eyes he might cry or be tempted to say something bad. If you want to fake it so that nobody can know if you are annoyed, you can start breathing in and then out as you count, or focus on the main aim of the conversation and you will realize that your annoyance is subsiding and while doing all this, ensure that your eyebrows haven't changed their former position.

Raised eyebrows may signify attention request or demand depending on the question posed before the raising.

Demanding for attention with raised eyebrows is seen rude sometimes especially if it is coming from a child to a parent or a younger person to an older on so you should be careful if you have this habit. Faking this raising of eyebrows when asking for attention, you may show attraction instead, when someone sees attraction in the eyes, he will give you the attention you want. This attraction can be done by raising your eyebrows to expose your eyes.

Submission can also be symbolized by raised eyebrows. For example, a person asking you if you are going to lend him money, and you raise your eyebrows. This means you have submitted to his request and he will get the money. But if you do not want the person to see that you are forcing this submission, you can as well lower your eyebrows, he will be confused and won't know if it is a yes or no or you can raise your eyebrows with the eyes looking up, this will tell the person that you are thinking about it.

Raising one eyebrow can also indicate cynicism especially when the other person is speaking inaccurately. The other person may feel offended if he saw you cynically raising your eyebrows thus to fake it, you can stay with your eyebrows normal but focus your mind on something else. When he is done talking, you greet each other and leave like nothing ever happened. Most of the psychologists use this faking especially to the clients who are so depressed and are speaking things that do not make sense, the psychologists even go ahead and nod their heads while the clients are speaking then they can paraphrase their words to get clarification otherwise raising one eyebrow to them will confuse them more and they will be annoyed that they are not getting the help they needed.

Pushing together your eyebrows and pulling up your forehead indicates relief. For example, you have been waiting for a whole day for some news from the interview you attended, then finally the results come and you find that you have passed. This is a great relief and you will feel your nerves calming down. This way your eyebrows will be pushed together, and your forehead pulled up. Anxiety can also be seen when the eyebrows are pushed together, and the forehead pulled up. You can fake anxiety especially when you want to get out of a boring meeting that you have by saying that you have to see a doctor. The show of anxiety on your face can get you the permission to step out.

Relaxing your face

A relaxed face is not a compressed face. A relaxed face can easily be seen by the facial muscles. The muscles are flexed, the eyebrows not clenched together, the forehead is not wrinkled or creased, the eyes are not tensed and the lips are full. All of these describe a relaxed face. If anything from the above is opposite, this means you do not have a relaxed face and anyone will be able to tell what is bothering you. To fake a relaxed face, you have to understand the following facial meanings;

A relaxed face shows control of emotions. It tells that you are in control of what is going on around you.

For example, you indulge in an argument at the office with the co-worker, the shouting is so high from your fellow worker that the other workers come in, just by the calmness on your face, the other workers will see your control of your emotions. They will know that you have the situation under control and it is not bothering you.

If you are a businessman and you want to show people that they can count on you, you must have a relaxed face. Relaxed faces show responsibility. Especially when there is a problem in the office and people are confused, by maintaining a relaxed face, people tend to see you as more responsible and they will be counting on you to provide the solutions to any problems arising. Most magnetic leaders are experts at this. They always maintain calm faces even when the going is so rough because they know people are counting on them.

When you are in control of things happening around you it is seen from your calm face. For example, you receive a call from the office that the workers are rioting, the police have been called to disburse then, but the situation is still rampant. So you decide to go to the office, with a calm face you call upon the workers, and they all stop whatever they are doing and start listening to you address their concerns. The calmness on your face will tell anyone that comes to that meeting that you have got control over your face even when deep within you know that you are not calm.

If you want people to respect you, make sure your face is calm especially during stress. When you are so hurt and stressed up, people will always see it on your face. But when your face seems so calm with no sign of stress, this will pull them towards you, they will respect you and most of them will want to emulate you. They will see a person that is a good example of control and can lead. A calm face will also make someone see honesty in you. When you are speaking to someone after a mistake has been committed, your face will let the person know if you are honest or not. For example in school, when something wrong has happened and the teacher calls you to the staffroom, the calmness of your face will tell the teacher that you are honest in whatever you are saying. So faking a calm face will help you get anything you want to.

Speaking In Balanced Tones

Tones involve the volume you use and the emphasis you place on every word. When the emphasis is placed on different words, the meanings of words change. When different tones are applied to different words, it changes the emotional influence of the words. For example, someone saying politely while joking 'you are stupid' it will sound funny and a joke, and emotionally it won't hurt you unless someone is speaking in a firm tone with a serious manner telling you the same thing. The emotional attachment to the first incidence and the second incidence differs because of tonal variation.

Trying To Fake a Smile

Faking a smile is not an easy thing to do especially when you are addressing a body language expert. It is likely to give you out when you are not so keen on how to fake it. The difference between a genuine smile and a fake smile is seen in the facial muscles. Some smiles do not display genuine positivity and their identification rests in the timing. How fast they appear and disappear matters most. A genuine smile is late coming and it takes time to disappear. A genuine smile is not instant. If you are speaking to a person and you want to fake a genuine smile, start to smile after he starts to talk to you and make sure your smile does not disappear too quickly. However, do not overdo it. If you wait too much longer for it to appear then hold it longer than it is supposed to before it disappears, the reality in it will be lost. Sometimes you may look weird if you are not doing it the right way.

You should make sure that your smiles appear in succession and are not even. Symmetrical smiles will let someone know that you are faking it because when you are trying to fake a smile you always want someone to realize it, so refrain from the even smiles with unbalanced time intervals for they will make someone know you are faking.

Supporting Your Head

How you support your head while talking tells more than you think. When your head is supported at the chin position horizontally with the chin lifted, this is a show of superiority. Most managers like sitting in this position in the meetings while listening to the views of the junior staff. This is an expression that they are superior over the others. Faking this is easy as long as you do not lose your focus. When you clasp your hands at the back of your head with the elbows spread out, this indicates that you are confident enough. You are confident about what you are talking about and at the same time, it signifies superiority and dominance. For example, a person is trying to send the message that 'I know this very well and I am the boss'. This happens mostly after someone has finished a certain project.

Sometimes clasping the hands at the back of your head while facing the opposite side of a person who is demanding something from you, may show submission. This is mostly seen when the police are making arrests. The police tell you to put your hands at the back of your head so that they can search you. When you comply, it shows you have submitted to the command or request that is being issued.

When you support your head sideways it sends different messages. You could be tired and you could just need some relaxing especially when you support your head with your eyes closed. It could also mean that you are indeed thought when you support your head with your hands on your forehead looking down. Supporting your head sideways with focus on the speaker and a smile can also indicate admiration. This happens mostly when people are on a love date.

Supporting your head by putting the hands on your head may show regret. This mostly is seen when football players have missed a penalty or a goal chance.

There are so many ways in which you can fake a body language and the above are just a few. You must realize that you have to at least fake a larger percentage of every symbol for one to believe it.

You can fake how to use your hands, your legs, your arms, your palms, your eyes, the way of speaking, your lips and so many other things to fit your objectives to fit the particular moment.

Chapter 7. Verbal / Nonverbal Communication

Verbal communication encompasses both spoken and written words. Words are a form of communication that humans have used to exchange their thoughts and messages, especially when they are not in a face to face setting. This is the most frequent form of communication used, and it is one that we have come to rely on the most.

One example of verbal communication involves public speaking, where communication is conducted and carried out verbally to groups of audiences. Other examples of verbal communication include your everyday conversations with your friends, family members, co-workers, clients, even random strangers you happen to meet as you go about your day. Verbal communication, in short, happens every day and it has become so routine we do it almost without actively thinking about it anymore.

As opposed to nonverbal communication which requires active thought. This form of communication has no words or sounds to rely on. Nothing but what you see with your eyes and what you make of it. When we use gestures, body movements, and facial expressions to convey our intent, that is a form of nonverbal communication.

What both forms of communication have is that they matter. They're equally important contributors to the overall communication process. You might even say that nonverbal communication is more important. The first impression you make on anyone is nonverbal. Even before the first hello and handshake. Take job interviews, for example. It cannot be stressed enough just how important it is to make a good first impression. Making a good first impression is absolutely critical during a job interview. From the minute you walk into the room, you are communicating with your potential employer through your nonverbal mannerisms. Your posture, facial expression, even the gestures that you make are going to be the clues that your employer is looking for when they assess you.

This same approach applies to other situations too, like meeting clients or conducting business meetings. The impression that you leave people with can be a big deciding factor in determining the outcome of your success. Saying all the right words, but with the wrong body language, is not going to get you the desired results that you seek.

Analyzing People via Their Verbal Statements

Our analysis and observation skills would be incomplete and inefficient if we ignore the significance of verbal statements. Verbal statements hold a myriad of keys into the doorways of our personalities, intentions, and emotions.

You can glean a lot from the words that you hear. Analyzing people through their verbal statements requires less effort and astuteness than that of nonverbal behaviors. We will take an in-depth look at how our words reveal our intentions, emotions, and personalities. I will include common speech clues that you will come across in your daily interactions with those around you. Let's delve into this significant aspect of communication.

Understanding the Relationship between Words, Behavior, and Personality

Everything you do (nonverbal) and say (verbal) speaks volumes about your personality. When you become adept at analyzing people, you will realize that there's a synergy between our actions, thoughts, and beliefs and that each aligns to provide a full picture about who we are. The words you use, even though it seems insignificant when compared to body languages, can actually tell a great deal about your desires, strengths, insecurities, and emotions.

How Words Reveal Your Personality

"Hey! Did you get taller overnight?" At first glance, this statement looks like a friendly banter, and it reveals no negative vibes. However, if you look at the statement from another perception, you will realize that it gives us an opportunity to glimpse the mind of the speaker. In this context, the speaker cares a lot about the height difference. How did we know that?

If you think about snakes all day because you are scared of them, then you might easily confuse a skink for a snake.

In other words, we notice the things we care about. When you observe the friendly banter, you will realize that the person may be concerned about his own personal height. This concern helped him to notice the height difference of his friend.

This statement could also stem from the speaker's insecurity about his own height. Remember, when it comes to analyzing verbal statement, you need to take into consideration the various factors at play, and this includes watching the body language too. In totality, both aspects of communication—verbal and nonverbal—are incomplete without the other.

Before we proceed, let's have a quick look at how you can analyze people through jokes.

Learn to Unclothe the Veil around Jokes

Two teenagers went into a restaurant. When the waiter came around to take their orders, one of the kids jokingly said, "I want anything that costs a million dollars." To a casual observer, it is a normal and bland banter. To an astute observer, this kid is worried about money. Perhaps his family might be passing through some kind of financial crisis, or his parents and loved ones might have taught him the importance of money.

There's always a hidden message in every joke. Therefore, learning to analyze these jokes will give you a glimpse into the speaker's deepest desires and personality. You should know that the words people use have a deep meaning, irrespective of how well-crafted the words are. A person might tell a joke to you without realizing he is revealing much more about his intentions. That is why it's easy to analyze those who make hurtful jokes to demean you.

Before we move to the next section, here's some advice: Never analyze a single phrase on its own. In order not to get incorrect results, try to observe the whole sentence, the manner in which the speech is conveyed, and the accompanying body language.

As a side note since we are talking about jokes, do you know the best sign that someone is intelligent? Humor. If you're looking to make connections with the smartest person in the room, find the one who is making others laugh the most.

Stories Are Powerful

It is easy to recognize a biased story, either verbally or in written form. You can effectively glimpse into the storyteller's psyche by listening to him or by reading his work. Here's an example for us to dissect:

From subject A's point of view: Last night, I was walking down a lonely street with my friends, and a large and muscular dark man appeared out of the neighboring bush and seemed to come toward us to attack. But he changed his mind in the last second and walked past us.

From subject B's point of view: Late in the evening, I was taking a stroll when I misplaced my keys in the nearby bush. It was already getting dark when I noticed I didn't have my keys on me. Time wasn't on my side since I needed to get home quickly to prepare for my date, so I searched and searched through the shrubs until I felt the keys. I jumped out onto the street in excitement and started running home. In my excitement, I nearly bumped into a group of frightened teenagers.

Both stories gave us different perceptive about the incident. The first point of view was from a teenager who didn't see the look of excitement on man's face. Rather, he emphasized the words huge, large, and dark. So why did he place emphasis on the physical attributes of the man who jumped out of the bush? Well, it's because that's the part that concerns him the most. He was scared because of the man's sudden appearance and physical size, and that had a huge impact on the story. We have a full and clearer picture when you look at the other man's point of view, and that is the power of perception in stories.

So when someone tells you a story, I want you to dissect the story and take note of the emphasized points of the story. By doing this, you will know how to analyze people effectively.

Common Word Clues You Need to Know

Words are like doorways to the mind. Words are often used to analyze people's thought processes, and the closest you can get to understanding someone's thoughts depends on your ability to decipher and listen to the words he speaks. Words that reveal a person's thoughts are referred to as word clues.

These word clues increase your chances of analyzing and predicting people's behavioral patterns via the words they speak or write. Word clues alone can't determine a person's personality, but they do provide us with an insight into an individual's behavioral characteristics and thought processes. You can draw your hypotheses from world clues and make a conclusion by taking notice of the other aspects of communication.

An Insight into How the Brain Process Works

There's something we have all come to agree on: the human brain is very efficient. We only use verbs and nouns when we think.

For instance, "I walked" or "I jumped." Adjectives, adverbs, and other parts of speech are added during the latter phase of converting thoughts into written language or spoken words. The words that we add at this stage provide an insight into who we are and what we are thinking.

The basic and simple sentence consists of only a subject and a verb. For example, the verbal statement "I walked" consists of only the pronoun I (subject) and the object that is the verb "walked". Any other word added to this basic sentence only modifies the action of the verb and the quality of the noun. These deliberate additions or modifications provide an insight into the behavioral characteristics and personality of the writer or speaker.

Word clues help us to make behavioral guesses or develop hypotheses regarding the personality of others. Take a look at the verbal statement "I quickly walked." The word clue in this sentence is quickly because it serves as a modification of the verb walked. This word clue infused a sense of urgency into the statement, but it did not give us a reason why. An individual can "quickly walk" because of the urgency of an appointment.

People who utilize this phrase are regarded as meticulous. Meticulous people are reliable and abhor being late for an appointment since they respect societal norms and want to live up to expectations. These set of individuals will also make good employees since they don't want to disappoint their employees.

Conversely, you can also quickly walk when in a dark and lonely area with a bad reputation. Bad weather could also be the reason why you quickly walk.

In summary, people might make use of the word clue quickly walk for a variety of reasons. It's important to always read verbal statements in relation to the circumstance surrounding the speaker or writer.

Word Clues You Need to Know

"I Labored Hard to Accomplish My Dreams"

The clue in this sentence is labored hard, and it shows that the person's dreams were difficult to accomplish. Perhaps it took him longer and harder to accomplish this particular dream as compared to the other goals he has accomplished. When we delve deeper, you will discover that the word clue labored suggests the person holds the belief that dedication and hard work can produce great result.

"I Bagged Another Contract"

The word clue is another, and it reveals that the speaker or writer has won so many contracts and this is just the latest accomplishment. From the above sentence, you can deduce that the speaker wants everyone who cared to listen to know that he won so many awards. He is trying to bolster his self-image by appearing successful. To an astute observer, this person seems self-conscious about what others think. More so, he needs the adulation of others to boost his self-esteem. Others who noticed this character weakness might try to exploit it for their personal gains.

"Jim and I Remained Friends"

The word clue in this sentence is remained. From the sentence, you can deduce that the speaker and Jim have gone through trying times. Perhaps the fabric of their friendship has gone through different difficult situations. They probably weren't supposed to be friends under normal circumstances. The speaker is trying to defend why she remained friend with Jim. The speaker doesn't feel convinced about her choice and, therefore, feels the need to defend her decision.

"I Patiently Sat through the Meeting"

Here, the word clue patiently holds a plethora of hypotheses. For instance, the speaker might be bored with the lecture but felt obligated to sit through it for various reasons. Perhaps the speaker had to use the restroom but felt self-conscious or trapped from standing up to go to the restroom. You could also deduce from the statement that she might have had an urgent appointment somewhere else.

Gauging from this statement, we can accurately say the speaker is someone who adheres to social etiquette and norms, irrespective of other pressing needs. Those with no social boundaries would have left the lecture to attend to any other issue that needed their attention. People with social boundaries like the speaker would make good employees since they know how to follow the rules and to respect authority.

Conversely, those who leave during the lecture to attend to other pressing needs are perfect candidates for jobs that require out-of-the-box thinking.

"I Decided to Buy That Dress"

The modifier or world clue here is decided. It indicates that the speaker weighed several options before settling for that particular dress. This statement shows us that the speaker is not impulsive. Rather, she weighs her options and takes the most logical step. More so, there's a high chance our speaker is an introvert since introverts tend to weigh their options before taking a step.

It's not a sure analysis, but a hypothesis about the speaker's personality. Conversely, an impulsive person would say, "I just bought that dress." The word clue just represents an impulsive decision.

"I Did the Right Thing"

The word clue, 'right', suggests that the speaker struggled with a moral or ethical dilemma before arriving at the decision. This verbal statement suggests that the person has a solid strength of character to make the best and just decision in the face of overwhelming opposing views.

As indicated by specialists, a significant segment of our correspondence is nonverbal. Consistently, we react to thousands on nonverbal signals and practices including stances, outward appearance, eye stare, motions, and manner of speaking. From our handshakes to our haircuts, nonverbal subtleties uncover what our identity is and sway how we identify with other individuals.

Much of the time, we impart data in nonverbal ways utilizing gatherings of practices. For instance, we may consolidate a scowl with crossed arms and unblinking eye stare to demonstrate dissatisfaction.

9 Types of Nonverbal Communication

1. Outward appearances

Outward appearances are answerable for an immense extent of nonverbal correspondence. Think about how much data can be passed on with a grin or a scowl. The expression on an individual's face is regularly the main thing we see, even before we hear what they have to say.

2. Motions

Purposeful developments and sign are a significant method to impart importance without words. Basic motions incorporate waving, indicating, and utilizing fingers to show numeric sums. Different motions are subjective and identified with culture.

In court settings, legal advisors have been known to use diverse nonverbal sign to endeavor to influence legal hearer sentiments. A lawyer may look at his watch to propose that the contradicting attorney's contention is monotonous or may even feign exacerbation at the declaration offered by an observer trying to undermine their believability. These nonverbal signs are viewed as being so ground-breaking and powerful that a few judges even spot restrains on what sort of nonverbal practices are permitted in the court.

3. Paralinguistics

Paralinguistics alludes to vocal correspondence that is isolated from real language. This incorporates factors, for example, manner of speaking, commotion, affection, and pitch. Consider the amazing impact that manner of speaking can have on the importance of a sentence. When said in a solid manner of speaking, audience members may translate endorsement and excitement. Similar words said in a reluctant manner of speaking may pass on objection and an absence of intrigue.

Consider all the various ways that basically changing your manner of speaking may change the significance of a sentence. A companion may ask you how you are getting along, and you react with the standard "I'm fine," yet how you really state those words may uncover a huge measure of how you are truly feeling. A virus manner of speaking may propose that you are not fine, however you don't wish to examine it. A brilliant, cheerful manner of speaking will uncover that you are really doing very well. A grave, sad tone would demonstrate that you are something contrary to fine and that maybe your companion ought to ask further.

4. Non-verbal communication and Posture

Stance and development can likewise pass on a lot of data. Research on non-verbal communication has developed essentially since the 1970's, however well-known media have concentrated on the over-translation of protective stances, arm-intersection, and leg-crossing, particularly subsequent to distributing Julius Fast's book Body Language.

While these nonverbal practices can show emotions and demeanors, look into proposes that non-verbal communication is unquestionably more unobtrusive and less conclusive than recently accepted.

5. Proxemics

Individuals frequently allude to their requirement for "individual space," which is likewise a significant kind of nonverbal correspondence. The measure of separation we need and the measure of room we see as having a place with us is impacted by various variables including social standards, social desires, situational factors, character attributes, and level of nature. For instance, the measure of individual space required when having an easygoing discussion with someone else as a rule differs between 18 inches and four feet. Then again, the individual separation required when addressing a horde of individuals is around 10 to 12 feet.

6. Eye Stare

The eyes assume a significant job in nonverbal correspondence and such things as looking, gazing and flickering are significant nonverbal practices. At the point when individuals experience individuals or things that they like, the pace of flickering increments and understudies expand. Taking a gander at someone else can demonstrate a scope of feelings including threatening vibe, intrigue, and fascination.

Individuals likewise use eye stare as a way to decide whether somebody is being straightforward. Typical, watchful gaze contact is frequently taken as a sign that an individual is coming clean and is dependable. Tricky eyes and a failure to keep in touch, then again, is regularly observed as a marker that somebody is lying or being tricky.

7. Haptics

Imparting through touch is another significant nonverbal conduct. There has been a generous measure of research on the significance of touch in earliest stages and early youth. Harry Harlow's great monkey concentrate showed how denied touch and contact obstructs advancement. Infant monkeys raised by wire moms experienced changeless shortfalls in conduct and social cooperation. Contact can be utilized to impart fondness, commonality, compassion, and different feelings.

In her book Interpersonal Communication: Everyday Encounters, writer Julia Wood composes that touch is likewise regularly utilized as an approach to impart both status and power. Analysts have discovered that high-status people will in general attack other individuals' close to home space with more prominent recurrence and force than lower-status people. Sex contrasts additionally assume a job in how individuals use contact to impart meaning.

Ladies will in general use contact to pass on care, concern, and nurturance. Men, then again, are bound to utilize contact to declare power or command over others.

8. Appearance

Our decision of shading, garments, hairdos, and different elements influencing appearance are additionally viewed as a method for nonverbal communication. Research on shading brain science has shown that various hues can inspire various temperaments. Appearance can likewise change physiological responses, decisions, and understandings. Simply think about all the unpretentious decisions you rapidly make about somebody dependent on their appearance. These initial introductions are significant, which is the reason specialists recommend that activity searchers dress suitably for interviews with potential businesses.

Specialists have discovered that appearance can assume a job in how individuals are seen and even the amount they gain. One 1996 study found that lawyers who were evaluated as more alluring than their friends earned almost 15 percent more than those positioned as less appealing. Culture is a significant impact on how appearances are judged. While slenderness will in general be esteemed in Western societies, some African societies relate full-figured bodies to better wellbeing, riches, and economic wellbeing.

9. Relics

Items and pictures are likewise apparatuses that can be utilized to convey nonverbally. On an online gathering, for instance, you may choose a symbol to speak to your character on the web and to impart data about what your identity is and the things you like. Individuals regularly invest a lot of energy building up a specific picture and encircle themselves with articles intended to pass on data about the things that are essential to them. Outfits, for instance, can be utilized to transmit an enormous measure of data about an individual. A fighter will wear exhausts, a police officer will wear a uniform, and a specialist will wear a white sterile jacket. At a simple look, these outfits tell individuals what an individual accomplishes professionally.

Chapter 8. How to Detect Lies

Imagine a world where people say the first thing that comes to mind, a world where you told the truth to everyone you talked with.

For example, let's say you took one look at your boss early in the morning only for you to tell him he looks like a weakling.

Or imagine yourself as a salesperson telling a customer how firm and perky her breasts are or a woman telling her male neighbor how nice and tight his butt is.

What do you think would be the result? Peace or chaos? Before I answer that, here's another scenario most people are quite familiar with: your spouse turns around in front of the mirror and asks, "Does this dress make me look fat?" Even if the dress does make her look fat, I know most men will say something along this line, "No, it doesn't, it's probably the mirror playing tricks on you."

So why do we opt to lie or gloss over some important facts? Well, it is to avoid chaos. As we grow older, we have learned the art of deceit to grease our interactions with others and help us maintain healthy social interactions. We know how much the cold, hard truth hurts sometimes, and it's no wonder research supports the fact that social liars are more popular than those who repeatedly say the truth.

This type of lie is referred to as a white lie since we often know the other person is trying not to hurt our feelings.

So, what about the malicious lies people tell in order to deliberately deceive others for their personal gain? This is what we are going to focus our attention on. We will take a look at the common clues malicious liars give when they lie or withhold the truth. Before we explore these common deceptions cues, I want you to understand why it's so important to study deception signals.

You and I deserve to know the truth. Society functions on the ability to trust people's words, that people will choose to abide by their words. If it didn't, society would descend into chaos, relationships would have a very short life, there would be no commerce, and parents and children would not trust each other.

In as much as we will sometimes use the white lie to avoid chaos, society also depends on honesty because we would all suffer in the absence of the truth.

Millions of people paid the price with their lives when Adolf Hitler lied to Neville Chamberlain. When Bill Clinton lied, it destroyed the reputation he had built over the years. When Richard Nixon lied, it nearly broke the steadfast loyalty and confidence of the American citizens to their country. Truth is, undoubtedly, essential in all relations, be it professional or personal.

We are lucky that people speak the truth most of the time and most of the lies we come across are usually social or white lies. When it comes to crucial matters, it is essential for us to assess the truth of what we are told.

It is not always easy finding the truth. For millennia, people had to rely on the use of torture devices to get the truth from those suspected of deception. Today, people have learned how to analyze handwriting and voice and use the polygraph test to know the truth.

Still, even with our advanced techniques, there are a lot of concerns about the accuracy of these methods. You may think you have little chance at succeeding when these modern deception analysis techniques can still fail. Don't be discouraged. With practice, you will become better at reading these deceptions cues.

After all, it is impossible to totally conceal deception.

Why Lying Is Difficult

Practice makes perfect, and most people have spent a good amount of time practicing and honing their lying skills. We have learned how to lie from an early age, and we've done it so often that we have become good at it.

Despite our perceived skills of deception, we still give off nonverbal cues that betray our innermost emotions to the astute observer.

For instance, people tend to smile less when they lie. This is contrary to the popular misconception that we smile more when we lie.

The difficulty in deception is that the subconscious mind gives contrary signals to our verbal statements. That is why it is so easy to catch someone who's not experienced in deception. On the other hand, actors, politicians, and public figures have learned how to refine their body gestures to the level where it's difficult to catch them in a lie. They tend to restrict their gestures in order not to reveal negative or positive gestures when they lie.

Researchers have discovered that it is easier to lie over the phone or an email. It is also easy to lie when part of your body is obscured from the interviewer or interrogator. It is no surprise that law enforcement agencies place their suspect on a chair in the open in a bid to have an unrestricted view of their body language.

How to Detect Deception

People give off different types of signals that reveal deception. Some of these signals are so subtle that even veteran body language readers might miss out on them if they don't know where to look. Some signals are insignificant unless you study them in clusters before you can get an accurate analysis.

In some cases, you will be looking for signals of lies of omission— looking for the hidden piece of information. Other times, you will be searching for lies of commission—verbal statements or actions that are inconsistent with the rest of the message.

Sometimes you won't have access to these deception clues since you might be communicating with the other person via an email or a phone call.

Variables such as ethnicity, gender, and cultural background can also influence how you detect nonverbal deception cues. Let's examine the major signs of deception in people.

Study the Body Language

Every part of the human body betrays our true feelings. By studying the arms, legs, eyes, nose, and torso, you can effectively deduce if someone is lying.

Liars Will Try to Avoid Eye Contact

When lying, people often avert their eyes in order not to betray their true emotions. They often do everything in their power to avoid looking at you since they think their lies will be uncovered through their eyes.

Conversely, people often give you their full attention and concentration when they tell the truth.

Restricted Body Movement

The arms and feet are great indicators of negative emotions, like deceit. It is easy to detect the gestures created by these body parts.

When someone is lying, they tend to be less expressive with their arms or hands. This means they are conscious about exposing themselves.

Have you ever noticed your arm movements when you are passionate about something? Your arms will wave all around as you try to emphasize your point.

When you notice a person sitting with his legs and arms close to his body, it's a sign that he's keeping something in. Watch out for unnatural hand and arm gestures. People who lie often try to overcome their restricted body gestures by using their gestures to convince us of the honesty of their verbal statement.

Involuntary Cover-Up

When the person's hand goes straight to the face when making a statement or responding to a question, it is a clear sign of deceit. Liars often cover their mouth while speaking as if they don't believe what they are saying.

Watch Out for Contradictions and Consistencies

In this section, we will take an in-depth look at the correlations between verbal statements and the accompanying body language.

From obvious contradictions, such as shaking your head from side to side while saying yes, to a more subtle form of contradiction, such as a pursed lip, you will learn how to accurately interpret these signals.

You will see that these signs occur both at the conscious and subconscious level. You will notice when people make a conscious effort to embellish their points through their forced gestures and off-timing.

You will also learn how to read people's initial reaction expressions. This is the initial expression you notice on people's faces before they mask it with other body language. Even if you can't read the fleeting initial expression, it is usually an indication that someone had something to hide.

Observe the Timing

Timing is everything when detecting deception. For example, if a person's head begins to shake in an affirmative direction before the words come out, then there's a high chance he's telling the truth. But if the person's head shakes after the point is made, it is a sign that the person is trying to demonstrate conviction.

Watch out for the arm and hand movements that demonstrate a point after it's been made. This gesture is an afterthought, and it's the work of a shoddy liar. These arms and hands movements won't only start late but also seem mechanical and in war with the "verbal" statement. Someone who is truly convicted about his statement will nod or shake the head in tune with every point he makes.

Be aware that a mechanical nodding when there's no point to emphasize is a sign of deception.

Sniff Out the Contradictions

Timing is crucial, but we need to pay more attention to contradictions between verbal and nonverbal cues. The woman who smiles while saying, "I hate you" is sending a contradictory signal. There's an obvious disharmony between her facial expression and verbal statement. Another example is a man telling his girlfriend or spouse he loves her while clenching his fists. Similarly, the gesture and the verbal statement are not in harmony.

Study the Timing of the Emotion

It is also difficult to fake the timing of emotions. For you to detect deception, carefully observe the timing of the emotions, and you will never be fooled. A fake emotion is not spontaneous; there's usually a delay in the onset of the emotion. The fake emotion lasts longer than normal and ends abruptly.

Let's take the emotion of surprise to paint this point. The surprise emotion is always fleeting, and it is a fake response if it lasts too long. So when people feign surprise, they usually keep the surprised face longer than usual.

The Unhappy Smile

Here's another contradiction you need to watch out for. I briefly touched this aspect when I explained the concept of smiles. I elaborated on the difference between fake and real smiles and how the former is limited to only the mouth area. When you pay close attention, you will notice that most deception signals are restricted to the mouth region.

Interpersonal Interactions

You need to consider a lot of factors when searching for signs of deception in people. Take a look at their posture in relation to the environment. Observe their stance to see if it's defensive or offensive. Research shows that guilty people are likely to go on the defensive since they feel they are boxed in. So let's examine the types of cues you will get from someone who's on the defensive.

The Head Shift

When people are not comfortable with their utterance or what they are hearing, they often shift their head away from the one they are talking to. This is an attempt to create a gap from the source of the discomfort. However, you will move your head toward the other person if you are comfortable and secure in your actions.

Take note of the slight conscious withdrawal or pronounced jerking of the head during a conversation. This is an indication of deception or a cover-up. Mind you, never confuse this action with a slight tilt of the head to the side. This gesture occurs when we hear something of interest. It could also function as a vulnerable position.

Check the Posture

Deception breeds insecurity in people, and this is reflected in the body posture. When an individual feels confident or sure about a situation, he sits up straight or stands erect. This also indicates how people feel about themselves.

Liars become unsure of themselves, and it's reflected in their hunched-over body posture. On the other hand, those who are confident about what they are saying will stand straight and walk briskly. You should know that this is not really an effective sign of deception since it is easy to consciously assume this position.

Those Who Walk Away

It is a human instinct to move away from those who pose a problem threat to us. You will never see prey willingly move toward a predator—it is not possible. This instinct is also an important sign for detecting deception. People who feel passionate and confident about what they are saying will often walk toward the other person. On the other hand, people who lie or deceive will angle their body or actually move toward the door.

No Body Contact

When we lie, we often have the feeling that the other person might see through our ruse. Hence, we shy away from any form of physical contact that might betray our real intentions. It is an important sign of deception. The liar will rarely touch the other person during a conversation. Since touch represents a psychological connection, the liar will unconsciously reduce the level of intimacy to hide his guilt.

No Finger Pointing

It's a fact that we all hate having people point their fingers at us. However, it's an indispensable gesture that we are all guilty of when trying to emphasize a point. It emphasizes conviction, and that's what liars generally lack. Therefore, a liar may not be able to use the finger pointing gesture to emphasize a point.

Verbal Content

It is possible to detect deception from verbal statements. The words we use can also provide a glimpse into our inner feelings or emotions. When people wish to deceive, they utilize certain phrase, words, or syntax that they think will portray the truth in their message.

An astute observer will be able to detect words or phrases dressed up as a lie. Here a few clues to detect deception in verbal messages.

When You Get Answers in Your Own Words

Take a moment to notice the way you respond to social greetings when preoccupied. When you walk into a classroom and someone says hi to you, you also respond with hi. At that moment, you are either preoccupied or not interested in making the effort to think.

In this same context, when someone is accused, he will reflect the question of the accuser out of fear of being caught. Why? It's because he's caught off by the question. For example, a furious parent asks, "Did you drink alcohol?" The liars will reply in the negative, "I didn't drink alcohol." You will notice that the word did in the question became didn't?

This is an important clue that the accused is lying since the guilty always wants to get the answers out as fast as possible.

1.   Liars Try More

Someone who is telling the truth will not try to go overboard in convincing you with his answer. A liar will go overboard to ensure that you understand his point in order to prevent further questions on the topic. And he will try to change the topic immediately when he thinks he has convinced you. He will use bold and strong words even if his evidence is fragile.

For instance, if asked if he has cheated in school before, he might answer with "I'm pretty sure I never did." Though, if he is trying to cover up for his past misdeeds, his response is likely to be more elaborate: "No, I would never cheat on a test."

2.   Watch for the Freudian Slip

We are all familiar with the good old slip of the tongue. We sometimes say one thing when we mean to say another. Most times, these slip of the tongue or subconscious leaks reflect our inner emotions or feelings.

For example, a baker who might mean to say, "I baked the cake all by myself all through the night," might slip and say, "We baked the cake together by working all through the night." Although Freudian slips are great indicators of a person's inner thoughts, their occurrence is unpredictable.

3.   Beware of Those Who Depersonalize Questions

Watch out for those who depersonalize your question since there's a high chance they are lying to you.

Let's say you asked a former employee, "Did you steal from your previous boss?" Watch if you get a reply along the lines of "No, I think stealing is the worst thing any human could ever do."

As you can see from the example, the liar has successfully thwarted the answer in an impersonal way. The liar might also go further by saying, "You know I abhor such things. I think it is morally repulsive."

4.   Liars Get Uncomfortable with Silence

Silence holds a lot of meaning, and for the liar, it means the other person is not buying what they are saying. They become more uncomfortable as the silence stretches far longer than necessary.

When you ask someone a question, observe if he supplies more answers without being prodded.

Here's a typical scenario you often see in movies: Mr. Peter is sitting before a police officer in an interrogation room. The investigator asks Peter about his whereabouts on the night of a crime scene, and he responds with "I was having a blast with my friends at the club downtown." However, the investigator doesn't acknowledge the answer. Rather, he stays silent and stares at Peter. As the silence becomes unbearable, Peter becomes nervous and goes on to add more unsolicited facts that actually implicates him in the end.

The guilty will always get spooked by the silence and will tell his story in pieces until he gets a verbal confirmation to stop talking.

5.   The Implied Answer Is No Answer

Here's a sign of deception you need to watch out for. Watch out for those who skirt around answering your question and instead give you an implied answer.

For instance, you are talking to a girl over the phone, and you asked her if she was gorgeous. If she proceeds to tell you that she works out three times a day, eats healthy, and jogs around the block in the evening, then she has given you an implied answer.

She is trying to circumvent the question by implying that she is gorgeous.

How the Words Are Conveyed

Here's a question for you: why do you think some company salespeople sell more than others in that same company despite reading the same sales material and selling the same product?

What makes the difference? I believe the answer lies in the way they convey their words. How something is said is just as important as what is said. So let's examine how you can use word delivery to detect deception.

1.   Study the Speed of Answers

A restaurant uses the speedy answer test to employ workers. Here's how it works. They will ask the employee if he has any prejudice against those from different racial groups or different sexual preferences. The longer it takes for the interviewee to answer, the lower the score.

Since the question has to do with beliefs, it takes a longer time for the mind to process. Therefore, someone who holds no prejudice or discrimination answers quickly. A prejudiced person will take time to come up with the "right" or dishonest answer—no one wants to be seen as prejudiced.

If, however, a prejudiced person is able to come up with a fast answer, the interviewer then observes how fast the rest of the sentences follow the initial yes or no response. Those speaking the truth will immediately follow their initial one-word response with an explanation. If the person is deceitful, the rest of the sentence will come slowly after the initial response.

2.   Liars Often Shy Away from Laying Emphasis

A liar will often try to limit his ownership and commitment to his replies. Pronouns such as us, we, and I are underutilized in his replies. When someone speaks the truth, he will often make use of the possessive pronouns as much as the rest of his statement.

For instance, a truthful person will reply affirmatively by saying, "Yes, I am." A liar may respond with a simple yes.

A liar may not place emphasis on words of expression, and he will often try to reduce ownership of his words.

For instance, a liar will quickly say, "It went great," instead of saying, "We had a greeeat time!" which is more expressive and committed than the former.

3.   The Mumbler

Have you ever noticed that kids tend to mumble their answers when lying? They will often look down and place their hands behind their backs while mumbling a lie.

Note that this response is not limited to lying; it could also reveal shyness. The mumbling gesture is also effective in detecting deception. A liar is likely to mumble his answers since he is unsure of his answers.

Someone who's passionate about what he's saying will increase the volume of his voice and speak faster.

4.   Analyzing Questions and Statements

If you are a keen observer, you will notice that questions and statements have different speaking styles. Let me explain.

When you ask someone, "What are you doing?" you will notice that the head comes up at the -ing part of the question. The eyes also widen at that last part of the question.

If the person replies with a statement that is styled like a question, then he is unsure of his statement and searching for verbal confirmation from you. However, if he replies with certainty, then he is confident and truthful about his reply.

Psychological Profile

These signs of deceit show how liars think and what characteristics are missing from a story that makes it fictitious.

1.   It Takes a Thief to Know a Thief

The way we see the world is a reflection of how we see ourselves. Someone who sees the world as a cesspool of corruption, lies, and greed may be full of these negatives.

Watch out for those who are quick to point out faults in others as they are likely to have those qualities themselves. That is why a con artist is always the first to accuse another of cheating.

If someone out of the blue accuses you of cheating or lying, ask yourself, "Why is this person so paranoid?" It is possible that this person is projecting their own qualities on you. So watch for these clues since they are often signs of deception.

2.   Another Dimension in the Story

Liars aren't always great storytellers; they often omit the crucial element when telling a story—another person's point of view. This is because most liars are not clever enough to add a third dimension to the story to give it more flesh. While the liar includes the other person in his story, he may omit the person's thoughts in the story.

This is not a clear sign of deception, but it is more believable if you include other people's thoughts in your story.

Let's say you asked your spouse about her whereabouts the previous night. In response to your question, she told you that she worked late. However, you are not convinced and decide to press further and asked what she had for dinner that night. Here are two answers she might give you:

"I didn't really feel hungry last night. So I came home and played a game with my roommate. She made a casserole, but I passed on it."

"I didn't really feel hungry last night. So I came home and played a game with my roommate. My roommate was aghast that I would actually skip dinner, especially her signature casserole dish."

Tell me, which version is more convincing, the former or the latter. Although both versions contain the same information, the latter adds another layer of thought—the opinion of a second party.

3.   Fewer Negatives in a Story

When someone tells you a made-up story, you will often notice the absence of negatives in the story. A liar will only focus on getting the story right. Therefore, he will stick to primary thoughts which are positives since negative is not a primary thought.

For instance, ask a friend about his vacation. He will cover both the positive and negative aspects of the journey, such as sunny and clear weather or the mix-up in travel bags.

Conversely, when someone makes up a story about their vacation, you will notice the absence of negatives in the story. There is a clause to this clue: "If the person is explaining about why he was delayed, then you should expect to hear some negatives."

4.   Rarely Believe Anyone Who Says This

There's no more obvious cue to detect liars than those who start their statements with phrases such as "To be frank," "To tell you the truth," "To be perfectly honest." Be cautious about believing those who use these phrases as the next thing that comes out, it is usually a lie.

Someone who tells the truth doesn't need to use these phrases to convince you—although some people have made a habit of using these phrases all the time, and it might not be an indication of deceit.

For those who don't use these expressions habitually, then it's a likely sign of deceit. So watch out if these phrases are not part of a person's verbal repertoire.

Also watch out for persuasive phrases like "Why would I lie to you?" and "You know I would never lie to you.

Chapter 9. Reading Thoughts

What He is Driven By

People are driven by various things. They will usually show what drives them by talking about it. For example, someone might say that he wants to go out to pick up chicks. Obviously sex drives him. Someone who frequently talks about money and making money is driven by financial security and wealth. Someone who talks about socializing a lot is an extrovert who is driven by having social interaction.

What drives a person can indicate what he wants from you. Read a person's language to gather clues about what he wants in life. His drive can indicate why he is seeking any sort of relationship with you, either professionally or personally. It also indicates what is important to him. If your goals align with his, then a relationship is a good idea. Otherwise, you may want to steer clear of this person.

What Feeds His Ego

Watch a person's ego to find out what feeds it. A lot of people are fed by accomplishments, such as making money or finishing a tough marathon. Some people are fed by flattery and being the object of desire. Some people are fed by sex and interactions with the opposite sex. What feeds someone's ego is apparent by what he talks about the most and what makes him smile.

Also, watch his responses to life situations. If a member of the opposite sex flirts with someone and his or her ego blossoms, you can assume that he or she has low self-esteem and requires lots of sexual attention to feel good. If he brags about his boat and other material possessions, you can tell that material success is what makes him feel complete.

If someone has a fragile ego that is fed by superficial things like material possessions and sexual attention, you can be sure that he has little confidence. The issues that come with insecurity are thus probably prevalent in this person. He will also do things to satisfy his own ego, and will chase after things and make stupid decisions just to keep his ego buoyed. Expect vices in someone like this.

But if someone's ego is fed by more solid things, such as his own accomplishments or the love of his family, then he is probably a secure and reliable person with healthy confidence and wholesome interests. You can trust someone like this to be a more solid companion in business or in your personal life.

What Stresses Him Out

Watch out for someone's stressors. Everyone has a source of stress. What a person complains about the most usually indicates what causes him the most emotional stress. If he complains about family, communication, commitment, and not always getting his way or not feeling loved may cause him stress. If he complains about work, his line of work and the tasks that he must do are probably not well-suited to his personality. If he seems to get quiet or upset in large crowds, you can assume that large crowds are not his forte.

Knowing what stresses someone out is very useful information. You can learn what to avoid doing around someone. You can become more sensitive to what someone does not like and also to situations that a person does not function well in. This is great information to know if you hire someone to work for you or if you begin dating someone.

What Pleases Him

People will go on and on about what makes them happy. You will most likely find out what makes someone happy relatively early in conversation. But you can also look for clues in what makes someone smile or what someone fixates on with dilated pupils.

This is also useful to know. You learn what you can do to please someone. This can make you a better lover, friend, or even employer and co-worker.

How Does He Behave Under Stress

How someone handles stress says a lot about how he will treat you when things get hard. Life can throw a lot of challenges your way, so you usually want people around who can handle stress well. If a stressful situation arises and someone literally falls apart or gets fiercely angry, just know that he is probably not a reliable friend during times of stress. He is also not a good prospect in a stressful line of business. On the other hand, if he is able to remain calm and collected under stress, he is someone that you can rely on in the future.

Chapter 10.   Understanding Intentions

It's All in the Eyes - Clues to Revealing True Intentions

When children are being evaluated for neurological challenges, one of the main observable points is their ability to maintain good eye contact. Although an intricate detail, the ability to lock eyes with someone else during conversation speaks wonders to the child's level of function. If a child is able to maintain direct eye contact throughout the course of their assessments, they are deemed high on the social spectrum. However, the inability to maintain eye contact could be a sign of autism or even social anxiety. The eyes reveal small truths to the inner workings of our biology.

Typically, what is the first thing you look at when meeting someone? Usually, their eyes reveal aspects of beauty that are attractive to first encounters. Many even remember people because of the shape, color, and size of the eyes. We are neurotically programmed to be visual creatures who make associations through what we see. Generally, these associations are labeled by what we give off. Since every aspect of the body works in conjunction with the brain, how do our eyes communicate with certain receptors?

The Eye Meets the Brain

The retina is like the gatekeeper of the eye. Everything we see, through the exchange of light, passes through the retina and is then transferred to two different aspects of the eye: rods which manage our ability to see at night, and cones which handle our daily vision activities such as color translation, reading, writing, and scanning. Various neurons travel throughout the eye and communicate with different functions within the eye to carry unique signals. These signals are then carried through the optic nerve into the cerebral cortex. The cerebral cortex is like the movie theatre of the brain. It controls our visual receptors that are responsible for perception, memory, and thoughts. When our eye sees something pleasurable, researchers have discovered that the pupil actually expands. This phenomenon proves that what we see is how we think. Through this, we can formulate opinions, draw conclusions, and even interpret body movements.

There are certain concrete directions carried out by the eyes that indicate true intentions:

- Right glance: This is used to remember something, maybe a name, face, song, or book.

- Left glance: This is used to remember physical features such as color, shape, texture, and other visual stimulants.
- Glancing downward in a right position: This controls our imagination and what we believe something to be like.
- Glancing downward towards the left: Inner communication, the conversations we have with the self.

The way our eyes work with the brain and perception is key to understanding body language. Since we use every aspect of our body to communicate, it is only natural that the eyes play a major role in this form of communication. Sure, the eyes may seem one dimensional to the untrained individual. However, their slight movements can indicate everything you need to know about a person. Let's consider a few examples.

Direct Eye Contact

Direct eye contact can mean a caveat of emotions. Surely, self-confidence is one of the primary indicators of locking eyes. When vetting for a job, recruiters will often instruct their interviewees to look the interviewer in the eye in order to display awareness. This shows the interviewer that you aren't intimidated and can take on any task. Similarly, animals utilize eye contact when interpreting dominance. For example, a trainer will often look a dog in the eye that he is training in order to establish dominance. By the trainer locking eyes and refusing to move, the dog will know to listen to his commands. Humans also communicate via dominant signals. Direct eye contact trumps fear. It shows that you are comfortable with the conversation, and it indicates interest.

In addition, balance is the key to everything. Too much direct eye contact could prove to be intimidating to the receiving individual. This intense stare could cause others to feel uncomfortable, with them maybe even questioning your overall sanity. Imagine engaging in a conversation with someone who never stopped looking into your eyes. Even when you looked away, their eyes were still locked on yours. Surely, you would chalk them up to be extremely strange. It's always important to be cognizant of what your eyes are doing as staring, in some cultures, could be viewed as rude.

Looking Away

When a person avoids eye contact, this is typically a sign of low self-confidence. The person may be uncomfortable with the conversation, person, or environment that they are in. In addition, anxiety surrounding social settings can make a person apprehensive to locking eyes with someone they don't know. Avoiding eye contact also signals inner conflict. Perhaps they are fighting against subconscious urges of attraction; therefore, they avoid making eye contact; or maybe they are hiding something that heightens their anxiety. This doesn't indicate that a person is devious or even untrustworthy. They may suffer from debilitating self-consciousness that overwhelms their disposition.

Dilated Pupils

The pupils generate intricate signals that identify even the smallest of changes within the body. Studies have shown that when people are presented with a challenging question, their pupils grow larger. When the brain is forced to think beyond its capabilities, the pupils actually become narrow, according to a 1973 study. The pupils are also key indicators of stress on the brain. Health care professionals will shine a small flashlight into the eyes of their patients in order to check the normality of their pupils. If the pupils are balanced in size and react to the shining light, the brain isn't experiencing distress. However, any imbalance could indicate a serious brain injury.

Dilated pupils express extreme interest, even agreement. When you see or hear something that sparks your attention, your pupils will dilate almost immediately. The same occurs when a person is shown a representation of something they agree with. In 1969, a revered researcher sought to prove the notion that the pupils' dilation can reveal political affiliations. By showing participants pictures of political figures they admired, the participants' eyes dilated. However, when shown an opposing photo, the pupils grew narrow; often snake-like.

What Our Visual Directions Indicate

The positioning of our eyes and what we choose to focus on during a conversation can speak volumes. For instance, glancing downward could indicate shame, even submission. When children are being reprimanded, they are often looking down to show their personal disdain for their behavior. In ancient Chinese culture, one typically looked down in a submissive form to show respect to those in authority. On the contrary, glaring upward indicated traits of haughtiness. It is often associated with being bored or not wanting to engage in the activity at hand. In addition, looking up signals uncertainty. Movies and television shows may depict a teenager taking a test and looking up because they are unaware of the answer.

Sideways glances are often cues for internal irritation. For example, when a co-worker you dislike walks into the room, you may inadvertently look at them sideways, simply because they are the bane of your existence. This can also occur when engaging with individuals who annoy you. The takeaway from the sideways stare is discontentment. When you see something that just isn't right, or even a sneaky individual, you may give them the side-eye. This demonstrates total repulsion for their attitude, reputation, or even their expressions.

Many would attribute squinting to being unable to see. While true, a squint can also mimic signs of disbelief or confusion. One may hear something and want more information. Thus, they squint their eyes while listening; it's almost as if they are saying, "I don't believe you...I need more answers!"

Stress can induce quick blinking which causes a person to go into a frenzy. You may notice a person rapidly blinking while moving frantically to finish a task. This could be accompanied by sweat or trembling. On the contrary, excessive blinking could be a subtle sign of arrogance. A boss, for example, may blink rapidly while speaking to an employee in an attempt to dismiss their conversation. This fast-action blinking essentially blinds the boss from the employee for less than a second, indicating that they would rather be engaging in something else.

A direct gaze paired with a lowered lid and head indicates extreme attraction. It's almost likened to a "come hither" invitation between mates. This gaze is heightened through sexual attraction and may even induce pupil dilation.

Inability to Focus and Attention Deficit

An eye nystagmus identifies how long it takes the body to focus on one point after undergoing extreme movement. If a person has a nystagmus lasting longer than 14 seconds, they may have challenges with keeping focused. One academic facility tests the accuracy of a child's nystagmus by spinning them a number of times and having them glance up towards the ceiling. The eyes then move rapidly, sometimes dilating, then narrowing. The longer it takes the child to stabilize is documented. They further engage in this spinning activity weekly with the hopes of strengthening their ability to remain focused on one thing despite many distractions. As they continue to grow a tolerance, their eyes will stabilize in a lower amount of time. The goal is to strengthen their ability to dismiss outward distractions which will help with attention deficit disorder. The movement of the eyes tells trained professionals exactly how much assistance a child will need and in what specific area. Aren't the eyes magnificent?

Our eyes open the door to many revelations of the self. You are able to gain psychological perspective on how you perceive yourself and others by a simple glance! Irritation, lust, attraction, and even doubt can be detected by paying close attention. Since the eyes have a direct pathway to the brain, it is only natural that they are the gatekeepers of the soul. By implementing these quick tips into your social life, you will have the grand ability to analyze a person in a complex manner. Of course, the eyes are also home to detecting deceit. As we continue to travel through our body language adventure, we will soon learn how the eyes can reveal the trustworthiness of an individual.

Chapter 11.   How to Spot Insecurity

When you spot someone behaving irrationally, it's easy to dismiss them as being emotional or dramatic. Very rarely do we stop to consider that perhaps this might be a sign of insecurity. Instead of analyzing their body language to get the full picture and trying to empathize with them, we either choose to ignore them, dismiss them, or even get annoyed if they're irrational behavior is affecting us directly. We don't pause long enough to consider that this behavior could be their way of trying to cover up their emotional insecurity.

Your ability to spot insecurity can be advantageous to you in several situations. Negotiation, conflict resolution, and even within a problem-solving dynamic. There are several reasons why insecurity could manifest. People can be insecure about their looks, money, power, and most of the time, these insecurities can be difficult to manage when you don't know how to identify them. Once you do though, it gives you leverage that you can use to connect with the person on a level which they can relate to. In a negotiation situation, this can be extremely useful in swinging the odds into your favor.

Being able to spot insecurity is also going to serve you well in terms of protecting yourself. Sometimes, these insecure individuals have strong, negative energy about them, and it is easy to get swept up in their emotional turmoil and become insecure yourself if you spend enough time around them. A lack of eye contact, the nervous pacing, hunched posture, biting of the fingernails in some cases, repeatedly touching certain parts of the body like the neck, and fidgeting are obvious signs of insecurity and discomfort. Aside from the obvious body language that they display, keep your eyes peeled for the following signs that signal you're dealing with an insecure individual:

- They Make You Feel Insecure Too - Their insecurity will be so strong it starts to rub off on you. You'll want to exercise caution here, since beginning to doubt yourself is going to make you easy prey to manipulators.
- Constant Worry - They're constantly worried that every decision they make is going to reflect badly on them. They express concern about not knowing what the right thing to do is. They ask you want you think several times, or even what you think they should do. They might apologize for being indecisive and unable to decide just yet.
- Showing Off - Insecurity could also manifest itself in a different manner, where the insecure individual feels a constant need to show off their accomplishments just to make themselves feel better. Constantly brag about their

amazing lifestyle, their wonderful shoes, their huge cars, and their elite education. All of this is done to convince themselves that they have it all in a poor attempt to feel better about themselves.

- Becoming Defensive - Insecure people become even more nervous, jittery and on edge when they feel like they are being ganged up on or pressured into deciding. They'll be worried about offending you or making you angry with some of the choices they make, but they may become defensive if they feel like they're being attacked.

- Frequent Complaints - There's always something to complain about when the whole world doesn't seem right to the insecure individual. They'll spend hours, days, weeks or even months mulling over the concerns and worries, and find it hard to escape that "negative funk" they're in, no matter how much you try to coax them out of it. Even when there's nothing to complain about, they'll be the ones to find something wrong.

- Indecisive Nature - They find it nearly impossible to make a decision and stick to it. They'll second guess, question, bounce from one choice to the next, and keep asking the same question repeatedly, almost as if they're having a hard time accepting the answers they're being given. Even if you gave them a possible solution, they'll reject your initial suggestion, but then come back and circle it again.

Mastering your emotions is essential to dealing with an insecure individual to avoid being easily influenced by their volatile, unpredictable emotional state. Compassion and empathy are especially important, what the insecure person needs is someone who can understand what they're going through. Not someone who is there to judge, criticize or ridicule. Compassion requires a balanced approach so that our negative emotions are neither exaggerated or suppressed when dealing with an insecure individual. This balancing act comes out from the process of relating our personal experiences with that of the suffering of others. Your ability to analyze their body language and read the unspoken communication that goes on is going to be your best asset in a time like this.

Insecurity is an emotional state that arises following a situation that is perceived as alarming or threatening. If the person confronted with this stimulus feels that their resources or skills are insufficient to manage and/or overcome the situation, they are likely to feel insecure. This emotion may manifest itself in the form of higher levels of anxiety, psychomotor agitation, allowing the person to feel unnerved but still able to mobilize extra resources to enable him to succeed. In these cases, insecurity has a protective effect in that it prevents us from making mistakes or taking unnecessary risks. For example, when one of the couples feels that their relationship is not safe, they can implement some strategies that, in their eyes, imply the solidification of the relationship, such as the promotion of dialogue, romantic outings or even psychotherapeutic follow-up. Similarly, when a worker perceives his or her place as being at risk of being laid off, he or she will seek alternatives to avoid unemployment. But both in one context and the other insecurity can assume a higher level of intensity, no longer having such protective effect.

In these cases, though is likely to be dominated by irrational beliefs, which grow spirally and produce a blocking effect. The person starts to live by what makes him insecure without, however, being able to find adjusted solutions. In the first example, this state of anxiety could translate into a set of behaviors that have both despair and nonsense, such as starting to search the partner's cell for signs of a potential extramarital relationship, aggressive and/or controlling comments, etc. In the following example, it could happen that the person would be so depressed that he would not invest either in the current job or in the search for the new placement, allowing insecurity to have the blocking effect.

What clues or signs are evidenced by someone who is insecure? How can we identify him?

The most insecure people are overwhelmed by fear, and as a result, it is usually more difficult for them to take an assertive stance, that is, they have very serious difficulties in expressing clearly and honestly what they think and what they feel. Within a group, both can strive to go unnoticed as they can make efforts to please everyone. In practice, they feel an intense fear of failing, of not meeting expectations, of not being up to it. There are people who are very confident in professional terms and who are more insecure in relational/affective terms. In the same way, there are people who feel safe and comfortable in the performance of roles related to effective relationships but which reveal serious insecurities in other areas of life. It may not be easy to recognize the most insecure people, especially if the analysis is superficial.

Sometimes it is easier for an insecure individual to recognize another who shares the same insecurities, as he is more aware and more attentive to certain details that will go along with the majority.

Chapter 12.   Personalities

Every now and then, we try to assess and describe people according to their personality what they display in front of others. At that time, we may ask ourselves "what is a great personality?"

And we also say that his/her personality may be like his dad. So, in our daily routine, we might talk about human personality which creates a long-lasting impact on another person.

Furthermore, an individual's personality is inclusive of traits and patterns which clearly influence their behavior, thoughts, motivation, and emotions. Personality is that thing which drives a human being to behave as he/she does. However, human personality also depends upon on the genetic factors which you show to the outside world.

What makes someone who they are? Each individual has their own idea of what type of personality they figure. That's why psychologists have categorized human personality into various types.

Other than the professional atmosphere, there are environmental factors that can play an essential role in the development and expression of human personality. Means from childhood till adolescence how kids are brought up usually depend upon on their parents and their styles. Indeed, different norms and expectations of the culture make a human personality unique and attractive.

Now, let's put some light on the major components of human personality which make a human being a perfect person:

Impacts human behavior and actions- Human personality is not just how we respond and act in certain situations. Rather, it has come up with more unique benefits according to your past experiences. Means it constrains us to act in a certain way which maybe you don't like.

Shows multiple sides- A personality is not just our behavior with others or with ourselves, but it is a combination of our own thoughts, feelings, emotions, social interactions.

Now let's talk about personality traits regarding an individual which make them unique and different:

- Openness
- Conscientiousness
- Extraversion
- Agreeableness
- Neuroticism

These five traits act as an ingredient to make the human personality.

Openness- Open people are highly adventurous and open in front of others. Indeed, they are very curious to know new things and always appreciate art, imagination, and good thinking. The main aim of open people is to add spice in their or other's life.

Apart from that, an individual who is not open has the opposite habits. They want to confine themselves to their usual behavior and habits.

Conscientiousness- The conscientious people are more responsible and are well organized. These kinds of people are independent, focused to achieve their goals, and well-disciplined. Moreover, they will not backfire any type of journey which comes in their life ever.

The people who are low in conscientiousness are more spontaneous and free-wheeling. They are very careless towards their life. This trait helps in achieving goals in school or college life and in the job also.

Extraversion- The people who have extraversion trait in them are very sociable, chatty, and draw energy from the crowd. They are very assertive and cheerful in social interactions.

Furthermore, the opposite of extraversion is an introvert who wants to spend time alone with less social interaction. Their nature is very shy, but they are perfectly charming in the parties.

Agreeableness- This trait measures a person's heart in the form of kindness. They are likely to be trusted by anyone and are very helpful and compassionate.

Opposite to that, people are cold and suspicious, and do not cooperate easily.

Neuroticism- These kinds of people take more tension and easily slip into anxiety and depression. One way or the other, they find things to worry about. Due to these factors, a neuroticism individual is linked to bad health habits.

Types of personalities

Have you ever considered why human beings do what they do?

Why people react to the same situation in a different way?

In your life till now, have you tried to understand anyone maybe your loved ones?

And how in spite of different natures you get along with people at home or at work?

Every individual is unique in his own from head to toe, and despite all that, it is very surprising to recognize any person's personality. Psychologists have boxed human personality into varied categories so that it is easy to identify. Moreover, all these personality types tell us how individuals perceive the world internally and how they interact with others in different situations.

As we all are different, and this difference makes our place and life more interesting. That's why some individuals get easily successful in their life but, some take time. Have you imagined that what happens if all the persons were the same?

To understand this, let me give you an example, just imagine a house is on fire and out of many people some are rushing towards the house to evacuate it, some of them are making arrangements of the ambulance. Other than this, most of the people call the fire brigade. In this scenario, if all the individuals will do only one job, then who will do the other arrangements. This is one of the examples of varied personalities which is very crucial to handle any situation.

Every human being reacts differently in the same situations which are required to live life. We are motivated by different personalities, their thoughts, actions, and reactions. That's why numerous humans choose their role models which they want to be like them.

Now the next question arises why it is essential to understand human personality?

Well from an academic point of view, it is very interesting but, if we talk about life then it is much more essential than academics. The better you understand yourself and the human beings, the more capable you become in dealing with different situations and become more successful.

Understanding human personality is a practical subject so that you yourself maintain your life, deal with varied situations, manage the issues, and most crucially manage and understand your own impact on another person's life.

So, being blind to your own personality leads to these things:

- Negativity inside us remains to unlock; which as a result, becomes a hurdle in getting success.
- We only focus on our weaknesses, not on the strengths.
- You can miss the opportunity to play with your strength and improve your negative traits.

And you also need to understand the opposite person, which then leads to:

- Understanding another person, you try to interact with that according to the situation.
- While understanding the whole personality of the individual, you cannot get trapped in their first impression.

So, it would be very beneficial to understand human personality which would lead to happiness, growth, and self-development.

Conclusion

Be consistent in your words and non-verbal cues.

Speaking with another person, we influence him, whether we like it or not. Sometimes we do it intentionally, for example, when we are trying to piss off or cheer up someone. Statements requiring a reaction may be as follows:

"You heard that ...", or

"This nasty Mel Gibson!", or

"You know what happened ?!", or

"I love you".

With our own statements, we can unconsciously cause a person to a variety of associations and reactions. For example, asking "How are you?" We never know what the answer will be. A person can take or pour out all his grief.

Our mood can also affect others. If we are happy, then everyone around us is also happy. We are sad—and others are sad too. Often we ask people to change:

"Get a hold of yourself!"

"Take it easy!"

In order to act more strongly, one must simultaneously with words produce actions convincing the interlocutor of the seriousness of your intentions. If you want to calm someone down, you should not take him by the shoulders and shake him with a cry "When will you finally calm down?". To do this, you must first calm yourself down. Parents of babies understand how hard it is, but even with children, it works. "You must be tired," is the way to speak, accompanying the words with a yawn.

In this case, you need to radiate peace of mind, speak quietly, make smooth body movements, breathe evenly. To give someone confidence, you need to act confidently. Acting this way, you give the interlocutor's mind a hint, an example: you show with your appearance that it is possible to attain the desired state. There is a mutual understanding on a personal level. When you talk about something, you analyze; when you act, you create impressions, sometimes very strong. Think for yourself: would you prefer to talk about a kiss or get a kiss?

If your words mean one thing, and body language and voice mean another, the person will prefer to listen to the non-verbal message. If someone shouts "Calm down!", You will not listen to the words, but to the feelings that this cry will cause. It is unlikely that you calm down, rather, on the contrary, you get into a little more nervousness. To do this, do not even need to be able to read minds.